5·95

TEACH YOURSELF BOOKS

BIBLICAL HEBREW

NTC Publishing Group

TEACH YOURSELF BOOKS

BIBLICAL HEBREW

R. K. Harrison
Ph.D., D.D.

NTC Publishing Group

Long-renowned as *the* authoritative source for self-guided
learning – with more than 30 million copies sold worldwide –
the *Teach Yourself* series includes over 200 titles in the fields
of languages, crafts, hobbies, sports, and other leisure activities.

This edition was first published in 1993 by NTC Publishing Group,
4255 West Touhy Avenue, Lincolnwood (Chicago), Illinois 60646 –
1975 U.S.A. Originally published by Hodder and Stoughton Ltd.
Copyright 1955 by R. K. Harrison
Library of Congress Catalog Card Number: 92–82508

Printed and bound in Great Britain by
Cox & Wyman Ltd., Reading, Berkshire.

AUTHOR'S PREFACE

BIBLICAL Hebrew may seem to present a number of initial obstacles to the aspiring student. Its appearance is strange to those unfamiliar with Semitic languages, and it lacks almost all contact with the grammar and syntax of Classical or modern European languages. The alphabet is unfamiliar at first sight, and some of the letters are apt to be confused. Writing vocalised consonants from right to left is strange to the majority of people; the ring of Hebrew words and phrases, particularly when guttural letters are enunciated, is equally unfamiliar.

Another difficulty might appear to subsist in the triliteral nature of most Hebrew roots, so that to a beginner they not only sound alike, but would also seem to require a considerable amount of mental effort to fix them accurately in the memory. Furthermore, the virtual absence of compound forms demands a separate Hebrew word for verbs which to us may express the same root idea, a factor which again appears to make for excessive memory work.

Many such ideas arise through a beginner's unfamiliarity with the language, *but the student may be assured immediately that his efforts will bring a quicker dividend in the form of an ability to translate the original than would be the case with Classical and other languages generally.* A further merit is that previous experience in language-study is not essential; in fact, it may even be disadvantageous, and the majority of students grasp the principles of Hebrew grammar readily when only the mother-tongue is known. It is true, of course, that the study of any language requires enterprise, effort and perseverance, and in this respect Hebrew is no exception.

All students welcome the comparative smallness

of the Hebrew working vocabulary. Grammatical forms are quickly recognised as schematic, and once the primary rules have been mastered, they can be applied with almost mathematical regularity and precision to produce the required parts of speech. The verb paradigm is remarkably unelaborate, with its two themes expressing completeness or incompleteness, along with their characteristic modifications, and contrasts favourably with the complex verbs of Latin and Greek. There are two genders only, and no case-endings of the sort found in other languages. Hebrew syntax has rejected the elaborate formulation of subordinate clauses for a series of simple sentences coordinated by the copulative conjunction. This has given simplicity and vividness to the language, making it a powerful vehicle for conveying fundamental spiritual truths.

These factors largely compensate for the unfamiliarity of the language, and are always encouraging to the beginner. The author has endeavoured at every stage to introduce the various principles as clearly and attractively as possible, and has stated the main rules of articulation and grammar before attempts are made to translate phrases and sentences. In the writer's teaching experience this has worked most effectively with beginners, as it appeals to the rational processes of the mind.

Of a number of current systems of transliteration, what appears to be the least complex has been adopted. The mass of detail which characterises advanced Hebrew grammars has been avoided in the interests of presenting basic grammatical principles simply. This procedure imposes obvious limitations on the work, which nevertheless, as an introductory manual, may encourage the student to master what Ewald described as " the eternal mother-tongue of all true religion."

INTRODUCTION

A CERTAIN professor at an English University is said always to commence his initial lecture on the Hebrew language with the words, " Gentlemen, this is the language which God spoke ". Since substantial portions of the Divine revelation were given through the medium of this language, it is disconcerting to encounter such a marked resistance amongst Christian students to the diligent study of Biblical Hebrew.

The present writer feels that one reason for this state of affairs is the complexity and obscurity of the bulk of grammars published in the last century, and the present book is an attempt to state the basic principles of what is, after all, a comparatively uncomplicated language, as simply as possible.

Since Hebrew is now the official language of the State of Israel, it has gained in importance during recent years, and this fact makes its study a matter of more than purely antiquarian or theological interest.

The student will have sufficient equipment to study the simpler prose passages of the Old Testament when he has mastered the contents of the book, and in addition he will derive greater benefit from subsequent perusal of such works as Gesenius–Kautzsch–Cowley, for the finer points of the language as met with in more advanced Hebrew prose and poetry.

This, then, is a book for beginners, and whilst the writer makes no claim whatever to originality of content or presentation, he trusts that the simplified arrangement of the material will be of assistance to students, and especially to those who are endeavouring to learn Hebrew through private study. The chapters follow the order observed by the majority of grammars, and for the first few chapters the Hebrew words are transliterated as they occur, to enable the student to grasp their pronunciation and inflection. Proper names and technical terms are fully accented when they first occur, but subsequently they carry the minimum of accentuation, in order to simplify the format. The Divine Name is left unpointed throughout, and certain phrases are repeated in the exercises in a manner similar to the Biblical idiom.

A pocket lexicon suitable for beginners is the Hebrew–English lexicon published by S. Bagster and Sons, while for more advanced study the Oxford Hebrew Lexicon (Brown, Driver and Briggs), or the excellent two-volume work, Lexicon in Veteris Testamenti Libros, by Koehler and Baumgartner, will be found to satisfy all normal requirements.

I wish to acknowledge the kindness of a Canadian scholar, Rabbi David Kirshenbaum, of London, Ontario, in reading the manuscript and making suggestions for the improvement of this work. I am indebted to the Rev. J. M. Wilkie, M.A., B.D., formerly lecturer in Hebrew in the Universities of Durham and Cambridge, for his kindness and diligence in correcting the proofs.

A number of changes in the arrangement of the material have been suggested by scholars to whom the book was submitted in proof, and the majority of these modifications have been incorporated, so as to make the book as useful as possible within its obvious limitations. In this respect I am particularly indebted to the Rev. Robert Davidson, M.A., B.D., of Aberdeen. My final acknowledgment must be to Mr. Leonard Cutts, Editor of the Series, for his care and consideration in dealing with the book at all stages of its development.

R. K. HARRISON.

CONTENTS

BIBLICAL HEBREW

CHAPTER I

THE ALPHABET

Form. Primary or Medial.	Final.	Name.	Transliteration.	Numerical Value.
א		'Aleph	'	1
בּ ב		Bêth	bh, b	2
גּ ג		Gîmel	gh, g	3
דּ ד		Dāleth	dh, d	4
ה		Hē	h	5
ו		Wāw	w	6
ז		Záyin	z	7
ח		Ḥêth	ḥ	8
ט		Ṭêth	ṭ	9
י		Yôdh	y	10
כּ כ	ך	Kaph	kh, k	20
ל		Lāmedh	l	30
מ	ם	Mêm	m	40
נ	ן	Nûn	n	50
ס		Ṣāmekh	ṣ	60
ע		'Ayin	'	70
פּ פ	ף	Pē	ph, p	80
צ	ץ	Çādhê	ç	90
ק		Qôph	q	100
ר		Rêš	r	200
שׂ שׁ		Sîn, Šîn	s, š	300
תּ ת		Tāw	th, t	400

The Hebrew alphabet comprises twenty-two letters, all of which are consonants, and whose shapes in the first instance were similar to the objects which they are supposed to have signified.

HEBREW is one of the north-west Semitic group of languages which also includes Phoenician, Punic, Moabitic and Aramaic. It has considerable affinity with Arabic as well. From a linguistic standpoint, Hebrew was probably at its best in the period which saw the composition of the historical books such as Samuel and Kings, and the pre-Exilic prophets. Aramaic increased in influence particularly after the Exile, and towards the start of the Christian era it supplanted Hebrew as the spoken language of the Israelites.

We will now look at the Hebrew alphabet in some detail, considering each letter separately, and noting the manner in which it is to be sounded in reading.

א must never be mistaken for the letter "a", since it is always a consonant. It is represented by a "smooth breathing" ('), and is similar in nature to the silent "h" in the word "honour".

ב is "bh" and is pronounced like a "v"; בּ is a hard "b" as in "bat".

ג is transliterated "gh", and is pronounced with a slight throaty sound; גּ is a hard "g", as in "get".

ד is "dh" and is pronounced like the "th" in the word "the"; דּ is a hard "d", as in "day".

ה is the letter for "h".

ו represents the letter "w".

ז is the letter "z".

ח is signified by "ḥ", the dot underneath helping to distinguish it from ה. It is pronounced like the "ch" in the German "ach", or the Scottish "loch".

ט is transliterated "ṭ", the dot underneath the letter again serving to differentiate it from a subsequent "t". It is pronounced as a dull "t" by pressing the tongue to the palate.

י is the letter "y".

כ is transliterated "kh", and is very similar in sound, though somewhat lighter in tone, to the "ch" sound (ח) above ; כ is a hard "k" as in "kept".

ל represents "l".

מ is the letter "m".

נ is transliterated "n".

ס is represented by "ṣ", to distinguish it from a subsequent letter (שׁ), and has a dull "s" sound.

ע is transliterated by the "rough breathing" ('), and is pronounced with a harsh guttural sound from the back of the throat.

פ is "ph", pronounced like "f" ; פּ is a hard "p" as in "peg".

צ is transliterated "ç", and has a sharp hissing sound of "s", like the "ç" in the French word "garçon".

ק is represented by the letter "q", and the sound is like a "k" or a "q" pronounced from the back of the throat.

ר is the letter "r".

שׁ with the dot over the right hand corner is transliterated "š", and is pronounced "sh" ; שׂ with the dot over the left hand corner is the letter "s".

ת is the equivalent of "th" as in "these" ; תּ is a hard "t" sound as in "tin".

It must be borne in mind that the sound for

'Aleph amounts to nothing more than the emission of the breath in preparation for pronouncing the word or syllable of which it is the commencing consonant. When it occurs within a word its effect is much the same as if we were to pronounce the word "re-educate", by pausing slightly after the enunciation of the first syllable, and then stressing the second "e" by a fresh emission of the breath. The sound for 'Ayin is as though one were clearing one's throat, without, however, uttering a clear, deep grunt. Many of these sounds are difficult to articulate, and this is rendered more complicated by the fact that we cannot be absolutely certain of the original pronunciation. Furthermore, our Western articulation is different from that in the Orient, so that each experiences trouble in attempting to pronounce certain words from the other's language. For example, the Semites had a liberal sprinkling of vowel sounds in their words, and seem to have been almost unable to pronounce two or three consonants together. Thus a word like "rhythm" would probably have been broken up into three syllables by placing a very short vowel sound between the "r" and the "h", regarding the "y" as an "i" in sound, and placing a further vowel between the last two letters of the word.

However, our primary aim is not to secure a pronunciation as near as possible to what the original is thought to have been, but to ensure the mastery of a working pronunciation adequate for the articulation of the language as printed. Careful attention to the table of pronunciation will enable the student to acquire a reasonable accuracy in representing the original sounds. The letters with a guttural quality should be enunciated most carefully, as this is not

always easy for Western people to master, to whom
the majority of guttural sounds seem alike.

In writing Hebrew we shall use the printed
"square" character, so that whilst we talk about
"writing" Hebrew we are actually "printing"
it. Care must be taken with letters which look
alike but which in fact have some characteristic
difference. Looking through the alphabet in order
we notice that whilst the letters ב and כ exhibit
some similarity, the ב (bh) has a small projection
or "tittle" at the bottom right hand corner,
whilst the כ is rounded off to make "kh". ג (gh) has
a slightly angular projection to the left of its base,
whilst נ (n) is square at the top and bottom, and
thus is to be distinguished from כ, as well as being
smaller in size.

ד (dh) and ך (kh, final form) are frequently confused at the start. The latter will be seen to come
below the line of writing, whilst the former remains
on it. Both must be distinguished from ר (r), which
is rounded at the top, whereas both ד and ך have the
"tittle".

The letter ה (h) is different from the guttural ח (ḥ)
in that the top is closed in the latter, a fact which
tends to be a source of confusion. The letter ת (th) is
unlike both of these in that, whilst it is closed at the
top, it has a "foot" at the bottom left hand corner.

Difficulty is sometimes experienced in distinguish-
ing between ן (n) in its final form (which drops a
little below the line of writing), and the letter ו (w),
which has a slightly rounded projection at the top
left, and also the letter ז (z) which carries a small
angular bar on the top, extending to an equal
distance on either side. Of the primary or medial

forms, qoph (ק) is the only one to drop below the
line. The letter yodh (י) must always be written
above the line, on a level with the top of the other
letters except lamedh (ל), which is the only one to
begin a little above the other letters. If the yodh
is lengthened unduly it can be readily confused with
reš (ר), and possibly with waw (ו).

Final ם (m) must be written as a square, and in
this way will not be mistaken for samekh (ס), which
is round, or for teth (ט), which, whilst also round, is
open at the top. Primary or medial מ (m) is open at
the bottom left hand corner. The letter ע (‘) has a
different curvature from צ (ç), or from its final form
(ץ), which drops below the line.

There are five letters which exhibit two distinct
forms, which we have designated primary or medial,
and final, in our table of the alphabet. These letters
are כמנפצ, and when they occur as the initial letters
(primary), or when they are found occurring within
a word (medial), they are written as above, resting
on the line. But when they constitute the last letter
of a word, their forms are altered to ךםןףץ, coming
below the line, with the exception of ם (m). This
latter, as we have already observed, is written like a
closed square when occurring in its final form.

Six of the consonants in the Hebrew alphabet have
an alternative hardened form, which one may produce by inserting a point (·) inside the letters themselves. The consonants thus affected are בגדכפת, *i.e.*,
“bh”, “gh”, “dh”, “kh”, “ph”, “th”, but when read
with a point (*i.e.*, בּגּדּכּפּתּ), they assume a hard sound
and are transliterated “b”, “g”, “d”, “k”, “p” and
“t”.

We have seen that all the above letters are consonantal in force. In ancient times the Hebrew words were written without vowels in what is called "unpointed" script, so that each word consisted of a group of consonants whose vowel sounds were supplied from memory by the reader. The Hebrews knew, from oral teaching and practice, which vowels were associated with the different words, and it was only after many centuries that a mechanical system of vowel "points" was devised, enabling the reader to pronounce any word without prior knowledge of its sound. Whilst a vowel-less text (*i.e.*, unpointed) might be thought to be fraught with difficulty for the student, it must be remembered that some systems of shorthand at the present time employ the same idea with excellent results in intelligibility. If we were to take, for example, the consonants BT, we should actually experience little practical difficulty in deciding from the context whether the word was BAT, BET, BIT or BUT, and the same would apply to more developed forms.

One of the stranger features of the Hebrew language in occidental eyes is the fact that, in common with many other Semitic languages, it is written across the page from right to left. It is frequently perplexing to beginners to have to commence writing the Hebrew characters from the right hand side of the page, but only a small degree of practice is necessary to become used to this procedure.

On the basis of the information which we now possess, we may begin to write some of the Hebrew equivalents of the English letters in our table of the alphabet. Let us take a number of English consonants, such as "d", "ph" and "l". To write this in Hebrew characters we commence at the right of

our paper and work in the direction of the left,
thus ←———— (l) **ל** (ph) **פ** (d) **ד**, making the word
דפל. What might appear to us to be the "last"
character (*i.e.*, **ד**) is actually the first one to be written
down, followed by the second, (**פ**) and third (**ל**) to the
left of it.

Now let us take a group of consonants and transliterate them into square Hebrew character :

1. nphš.   2. mwn'.   3. ph'rç.   4. ṭzṣr.   5. šyrm.

This would be rendered as follows, beginning to
write at the top right hand side of the page :

1. **נפש**   2. **מונע**   3. **פארץ**   4. **טזסר**   5. **שירם**

A similar principle applies to the rendering of
Hebrew characters into English, except that in
transcribing them the student will begin writing at
the left hand side of the page and continue to the
right in the ordinary way. For example, a group of
consonants such as

1. **הן**   2. **צדיק**   3. **חלמיסא**   4. **קארא**   5. **עלמות**

will be rendered into English letters as follows :

1. hn.   2. çdhyq.   3. ḥlmyṣ'.   4. q'r'.   5. 'lmwth.

Care must always be taken to form the
Hebrew letters correctly, and to avoid confusion in
transliterating those which are similar in sound or
appearance in English as well as in Hebrew.

Exercise 1

Practice in writing groups of consonants in English.

1. **אתף**   2. **בלנו**   3. **קטלם**   4. **שלחוזי**   5. **משלך**   6. **ערביט**
7. **זפשלן**   8. **פלוחי**   9. **צלעפא**   10. **זרגחם**   11. **תלטמעין**
12. **הוכלעים**   13. **חפעזיק**   14. **טיראש**   15. **שלקאלו**   16. **דפטאנין**
17. **עלישמו**   18. **סמטשב**   19. **כצפעיל**   20. **חזקהמש**.

Practice in writing groups of consonants in Hebrew.

1. ḥṭšm.   2. lph'š.   3. çrmyw.   4. ṣnṭhly.   5. t'ql'my.
6. sbhwy.   7. qphṣ'ṭç.   8. dh'rm'ly.   9. pmḥṭš'nwn.
10. krm'ṣphqy.   11. 'zw'ghn'.   12. ṭršdhmw.   13. bghlṣḫ'.
14. çhwghl'.   15. qmthwy.   16. 'nç'lyn.   17. ḥnbhṭṣ.
18. thç'nṣ'm.   19. 'myn'ṭw.   20. grql'myw.

CHAPTER II

VOCALISATION

Up to the first few centuries of the Christian era, the Old Testament was written in unpointed consonantal Hebrew, with the reader supplying the vowel sounds from memory. As Classical (*i.e.*, Biblical) Hebrew fell into disuse for conversational purposes, it became necessary to devise some system of vocalising the text so as to enable it to be read correctly without any necessary previous acquaintance on the part of the reader with the sound of the words.

This difficulty had been partly met in the unpointed text by the use of certain consonants to indicate the principal long vowels, the particular consonants being he, yodh and waw. In practice this was as follows :

ה signified â ; hence לה was read lâ

י signified ê and î ; hence לי was read lê or lî.

ו signified ô and û ; hence לו was read lô or lû.

To show that these vowel-letters had a permanently long sound in their pronunciation, the English transliteration is accented by means of a circumflex (ˆ). A knowledge of the context was necessary, of course, in deciding upon the correct word from the alternatives which these vowel-letters supplied.

When such letters are omitted in the spelling of words to avoid reduplication of consonants, the vowels are then said to be written " defectively," e.g., עֵץ for עֵיץ. This is commonly found in the Hebrew Bible.

About the seventh century A.D. a vocalic system was introduced by the Massoretes, a group of people interested in preserving and vocalising the traditional Hebrew text, and who derived their name from the Hebrew word for "tradition". The system consisted of vowel points or signs which were written in and around the consonants so as not to interfere with their traditional sacredness. We will now study them in tabular form for convenience.

Table of Long Vowel Signs

Vowel	Name	Transcribed	Pronounced
◌ָ	Qāmēç	ā	As in calm.
◌ֵ / ◌ֵ	Çērê	ē / ê	As in obey.
◌ִ	Ḥîrĕq (long)	î	As in morphine

Table of Long Vowel Signs (*continued*)

Vowel	Name	Transcribed	Pronounced
וֹ ◌ֹ	Ḥōlĕm	ô ō	As in tone.
וּ	Šûrĕq	û	As in mute.

Table of Short Vowel Signs

Vowel	Name	Transcribed	Pronounced
◌ַ	Páthăḥ	ă	As in mat.
◌ֶ	Ṣ^{e}ghôl	ĕ	As in then.
◌ִ	Ḥîrĕq (short)	ĭ	As in hit.
◌ָ	Qāmĕç-Ḥaṭûph	ŏ	As in top.
◌ֻ	Qĭbbûç	ŭ	As in shut.

The line on which they would be written is indicated to show their relative positions as coming either above or below the line. To acquire the correct pronunciation of the various vowels it will be necessary to practise saying them very carefully. One will notice from these tables that the vowel hireq has a long and a short form, and also that the same sign (ֽ) is used for a long "a" and a short "o". Whilst this latter may appear confusing, we shall shortly learn a means of differentiating between the two.

The three dots in qibbuç are written at a slight angle, whilst the yodh in full çere ('ֵ) and hireq (long) are written to the left of, and above the vowel point. Because the consonants yodh and waw are used with points to express the vowel sound, they are said to have homogeneous vowels, and in transliteration this is indicated by a circumflex accent placed over the corresponding English letter. Thus full holem (וֹ), defectively ('), is written "ô" as distinct from the alternative rendering of holem as "ō". Exactly the same applies to çere. In pronouncing long hireq ('ִ) and full çere ('ֵ) an attempt should be made to recognise the place of the quiescent yodh, analogous to the way in which the personal pronoun "I" is pronounced, when a faint "y" sound is enunciated at the end. The full form of these two vowels, *i.e.*, including the quiescent consonant as well as the vowel itself, is said to be "permanently long", since the form of such vowels cannot be shortened under any circumstances, as opposed to the "tone long" vowels, which are only long in virtue of their relation

to the tone or accent, and which may become short
in other forms of the same word.

All Hebrew words must start with a consonant,
and when vowels are added, each one is placed in
close association with the consonant with which it is
to be pronounced, generally directly underneath the
consonant. Thus, to write "bā" we would use בּ with
qameç directly under it, *i.e.*, בָּ. A more complex
word "bārā'" would be בָּרָא, the consonant preceding
the vowel in each case, so that it could not possibly
be pronounced "bāār'", which would need to be
spelled in a different way. When the vowel sign for
holem is used, it is placed above the consonant, as in
מֹר, mōr, or with full holem as in דּוֹר, dôr.

When holem precedes א, the point is placed on the
upper right of the letter, as with יֹאמַר (yō'măr).
When it follows the א, the point is placed on the
upper left, as in אֹבֵד (ʾōbhēdh). When holem precedes שׁ, the points coincide, as with מֹשֵׁל (mōšēl).
When holem follows שׂ, the points again coincide, as
with שֹׂטֵן (sōṭēn). The letter שׁ will be "šō" to commence a syllable, *e.g.*, שֹׁמַע (šōmă'), and "ōs" in other
places.

Exercise 2

(*a*) Transliterate into English as many renderings as
possible of the following vowel-letter combinations :

‏חולי‎ 7. ‏מימו‎ 6. ‏להלו‎ 5. ‏שה‎ 4. ‏כי‎ 3. ‏מה‎ 2. ‏לי‎ 1.

‏לומי.‎ 10. ‏סטו‎ 9. ‏נהמי‎ 8.

(b) Transliterate the following into Hebrew vowel-letters :

1. lâlâ. 2. lîlô. 3. lôlâ. 4. bhânâ. 5. môlû. 6. nêlû. 7. mûnê. 8. lêlê. 9. qînâ. 10. lînê.

(c) Write the vowels corresponding to the following vowel points :

. 9. יִ 8. יְ 7. ֶ 6. ֵ 5. יֵ 4. ֵ 3. ַ 2. וּ 1.

ֵ 12. ֵ 11. ֹ 10.

(d) Write the vowel points for the following vowels :

1. ā. 2. û. 3. ĕ. 4. ō. 5. î. 6. ô. 7. ŭ. 8. ă. 9. ê. 10. ŏ. 11. ê. 12. î.

(e) Write the following practice words in pointed Hebrew :

1. bĕn. 2. bēn. 3. gôr. 4. mēm. 5. ’ākhăl. 6. çâphôn. 7. ’îš. 8. mēḥĕn. 9. ’ĕmĕth. 10. qôṭēl. 11. ḥāšîm. 12. ṣēphĕr. 13. gādhôl. 14. hû’. 15. šûrĕq. 16. môlênû. 17. ‘âphār. 18. hî’. 19. ‘ênê. 20. ’ĕbhĕn.

(f) Write the following practice words in English, transliterating (ָ) by qameç :

עִיר 6. צָפוֹנָה 5. מִימֵי 4. שָׁלוֹם 3. אֲרִית 2. אָדָם 1.

כּוֹכָבִים 12. קָרָא 11. מַיִם 10. לָוּ 9. אֱלוֹמִי 8. בַּת 7.

כֹּפֶר 18. יָרֵא 17. עָצוּם 16. אֵלֶם 15. נַמְעוּ 14. יֶלֶת 13.

שׁוֹר 19. מָחָה 20.

CHAPTER III

THE SYLLABLE AND THE ŠᵉWA

A SYLLABLE may be defined as a unit of pronunciation which in other than monosyllabic words forms part of a word, and which contains one vowel sound preceded—and often followed—by a consonant. Two types of syllable in Hebrew emerge as a result, and for convenience they are designated as "open" and "shut".

An open syllable is one ending in a vowel, whilst a shut syllable is one which has the vowel shut in between two consonants. An example of the first variety is בָּ, bā, which consists of one consonant and one vowel only, whilst the second kind is illustrated by the word בַּת, (băth,) containing two consonants with a vowel in between. So the word שָׁמַר (šāmăr) has the first syllable (שָׁ) open, whilst the second (מַר) is shut.

Words in Hebrew are generally accented or stressed on the final syllable, and in transcription this is denoted by a small arrow-head over the stressed syllable, e.g., זָקֵן (zāqēn). When the accent falls on the last or ultimate syllable it is said to be Milra' (מִלְרַע means "from beneath"). But there are also a considerable number of words stressed on the

penultimate or next to the last syllable, *e.g.*, חֶׁסֶד
(ḥĕṣĕdh) and this accentuation is said to be Mil'el
(מִלְעֵיל means "from above", *i.e.*, above the end of
the word).   The accent rarely if ever falls on the
ante-penultimate in a word of more than two
syllables.

The tone or accent is closely related to the vowel
properties of the syllable.   An open syllable generally has a long vowel, but if it carries the accent it
can have a short vowel.   The word for "heaven"
conveniently illustrates this point.   The pretonic
syllable of שָׁמַיִם (šā-mǎyǐm), *i.e.*, שָׁ, is open and has
a long vowel, but the syllable carrying the tone or
accentuation (מַ) is short, although it too is open.

Similarly a shut syllable generally has a short
vowel, but it may have a long vowel if the accent
falls on it.   So with דָּבָר (dābhār) the accentuation is
milra', and whilst being a shut syllable it has a long
vowel.

Out of all this may be stated an important rule :

Any syllable which is shut and does not carry the
accent must have a short vowel.

In addition to the long and short vowels, there is
another variety of enunciation which is in effect a
very quick vocalic utterance, amounting in tonal
quantity to about half of an ordinary short vowel.

The ancient Hebrews called this hurried vowel-sound the "šᵉwa" (שְׁוָא from a root meaning "nothingness") to show its lightness of sound.

Attempts to illustrate its function in English are not wholly satisfactory, but an analogy may be found in the pronunciation of the word "banana". When we enunciate it, we do not split it up into evenly balanced syllables and say "ba-na-na", as the word is spelled. Instead we practically obliterate the first vowel "a" and substitute for it a hurried, blurred "e" sound as we press on to pronounce the second and third syllables. If this were a Hebrew word, it would then be transliterated "bᵉnana", the small superscript "e" signifying that very short tonal quality characteristic of the hurriedly pronounced vowel. Similarly the word "police" is not uttered as "po-lice", but the "o" again undergoes a change of sound in the quickness of pronunciation, and would be transliterated "pᵉlice".

The šᵉwa may be simple or augmented in nature, and in addition to the quick, light vocal sound there is also a silent form of šᵉwa. The simple šᵉwa, vocal or silent, is represented by a colon-like sign (:) placed under a consonant, while an augmented or composite form (ḥāṭēph) has one of three short vowels added to the left of it. These may be compared as follows :

Table of Šᵉwas

Sign	Name	Vocalised
ְ	Simple Šᵉwa	It may be silent ; or it may have a short " e " sound.
ֲ	Ḥāṭēph-Păthăḥ	Slight " a " sound, *e.g.*, חֲמוֹר ḥᵃmôr.
ֱ	Ḥāṭēph-Sᵉghôl	Slight " e" sound, *e.g* , אֱלֹהִים 'ᵉlōhîm.
ֳ	Ḥāṭēph-Qāměç-Ḥăṭûph	Slight " o " sound, *e.g.*, חֳלִי ḥᵒlî.

The difficulty which the Semites apparently experienced in pronouncing two or more consonants together perhaps explains the frequent occurrence of the šᵉwa in its various forms, some of which may now be noted.

The šᵉwa, simple or augmented, is placed under every consonant which does not have a full vowel of its own if the consonant is to be articulated, or if the consonant is not the last letter of a word. So the form נקטל (nǐqṭōl) would be incorrect as written, since the ק is pronounced, and thus needs a šᵉwa under it to ensure its vocalisation, *e.g.*, נְקְטֹל.

The simple šᵉwa is vocalic (or sounded) when it occurs under the first consonant of a syllable,

whether at the beginning (*e.g.*, קְטֹל qᵉṭol) or in the
middle (*e.g.*, קָטְלוּ qāṭᵉlû) of a word. When it closes
a syllable in the middle of a word it is silent, *e.g.*,
יִשְׁמְרוּ (yišmᵉrû), and is not represented by any
symbol in transliteration.

When two šᵉwas occur together, as in the previous
example, the šᵉwa which appears under the שׁ will be
silent, whilst that which is under the מ is vocalic.
A šᵉwa which follows a long vowel is generally
vocalic, *e.g.*, קָמְרוּ (qāmᵉrû), whilst that which comes
after a short vowel is normally silent, *e.g.*, יִכְבַּד
(yĭkhbădh).

Four letters א ה ח ע known as guttural letters
from their throaty pronunciation, take a composite
or augmented šᵉwa instead of a simple one. The
shapes of these have already been given in the fore-
going table. Like the simple šᵉwas, these augmented
forms are placed under the consonants, and are given
the technical name of "ḥāṭeph", from a word חָטֵף
meaning "hurried". א prefers hateph sᵉghol (ֱ), but
the other letters within the guttural class do not
exercise any especial hateph preference.

A few rare words which terminate in two sounded
consonants have simple šᵉwa under each, *e.g.*, יָשְׁקְ
(yăšq). A quiescent (*i.e.*, not sounded) letter does
not take šᵉwa, *e.g.*, בִּימֵ (bîmê), not בִּימֵ (bîᵉmê). The
final form of kaph (ך) takes simple šᵉwa inside rather
than beneath, *i.e.*, לָךְ (lākh).

An important function of the simple šewa silent is that it indicates a shut syllable, and thus the existence of a short vowel within that syllable. This enables us to distinguish qameç (long "a") from qameç hatuph (short "o"), since if the vowel were long "a" the syllable could not then be regarded as shut. Thus יִקְטֹל reads yŏqṭăl, not yāqᵉṭăl.

If two sounded simple šᵉwas come together at the beginning of a word in process of modifying its structure, or even appear to do so, the first becomes hireq (.) whilst the second is vocalised. This often happens with a preposition which attaches itself to another word, *e.g.*, with בְּרָכָה (bᵉrākhâ), to which we might wish to add the inseparable preposition לְ ("to" or "for"). Ordinarily we would expect this to be לְבְּרָכָה, but since it is impossible for two sounded šᵉwas to come together, the לְ becomes לִ (lî), hence לִבְרָכָה, "for a blessing", the point being taken out of the letter ב in the process.

The existence of a vocal šᵉwa in words has been held by many scholars to mark the presence of a " half-open " syllable, neither completely open nor yet fully shut. In effect this makes a syllable out of each consonant with a vocal šᵉwa, so that קְטַלְתֶּם thus becomes not qᵉṭăl-tĕm but qᵉ-ṭăl-tĕm, and יְלִידֵי becomes not yᵉlî-dhê but yᵉ-lî-dhê. It must be observed at this point that the vocal šᵉwa not infrequently retains the force of what in other forms of the word may be a full vowel, a fact which would be obscured if it were regarded as a silent šᵉwa simply marking a shut syllable, without any vocalic nature at all. This may perhaps justify the term " half-open syllable", which some authorities jettison.

Exercise 3

Transliterate and pronounce carefully the following practice words :

(a) 1. אֲדֹנִי 2. מִשְׁפָּט 3. טוֹבִים 4. יְקֻבְּרוּ 5. חָמֵץ

6. מַלְכְּךָ 7. חֲלַיטַ 8. עָמְדוּ 9. אֱמוֹר 10. גְּדוֹלַי 11. כֹּהֲנִים

12. יָדְמֵר 13. לְבָבָם 14. שָׁאֲלוּ 15. אֲנָשִׁים 16. אֱלֹהִים

17. הֶחֱטִיא 18. תְּנָה 19. אֲשֶׁר 20. מַחֲנֶה.

(b) Transliterate into Hebrew :

1. šᵉlômî. 2. yiqṭᵉlû. 3. dᵉbhăr. 4. bᵉnê. 5. 'ᵃlêkhĕm.
6. kᵉnă'ăn. 7. yārᵉ'û. 8. yă'ᵃzōbh. 9. ḥᵃzāqâ.
10. 'ăḥᵃrōnî. 11. hăḥᵃlôm. 12. 'ᵃnăḥnû. 13. mišmăr.
14. bᵉrākhăth. 15. ḥᵃzāqôth. 16. bᵉ'ênê. 17. 'êlāyw.
18. yă'ᵃsĕh. 19. 'ᵃdhăth. 20. bᵉkhôrê.

CHAPTER IV

THE DAGHEŠ

THE word "dagheš" is the designation applied to a dot placed in the middle of a letter, and means "piercing" (דָּגֵשׁ). There are two principal varieties, dagheš lene (or weak) and dagheš forte (or strong). We will first consider the principles underlying the behaviour of dagheš lene.

Acquaintance has already been made with six letters which take a point in their bosom to produce a hardened tonal quality. These letters, ב ג ד כ פ ת have this dot, called dagheš lene, placed inside them whenever they do not immediately follow a vowel sound. In order to remember the letters, a mnemonic word is made by pointing them thus : בְּגַדְכְּפַת (beghădhkephăth), and which at the same time illustrated the use of dagheš lene. The first letter ב has the dagheš because it is obviously isolated from any preceding vowel sound, since it begins the word. The šewa under it is vocal, and so ג does not take dagheš lene, since in this instance a vocal šewa, simple or augmented, has the same effect as an ordinary full vowel. ד again has no dagheš lene, since it follows the vowel sound pathah under ג.

We have seen that when two šewas occur together,

the first is silent and the second vocalic. Therefore, by our rule above, כ will of necessity have dagheš lene, since it does not immediately follow a vowel sound, the šᵉwa under ד being silent. פ and ת have no dagheš since they both follow a vocalic sound.

To summarise this we may say that dagheš lene is always found in the bᵉghadhkᵉphath letters at the beginning of a word if there is no vocalic connection with the previous word, and that it also occurs at the beginning of a syllable if the previous syllable of that word is shut.

Dagheš forte was perhaps so called because it hardens or sharpens the sound of the letters containing it, whilst dagheš lene indicated a softer or lighter degree of utterance. Dagheš forte has the effect of doubling the letter in which it appears, so that קַטֵּל would be equivalent to קַטְטֵל. For this to take place it will be apparent that dagheš forte must follow immediately on a vowel sound. When the letters yodh and waw appear as consonants they may take dagheš forte, e.g., צִיּוֹן (çîyyôn). The guttural letters א ה ח ע, along with ר, cannot be doubled in enunciation very well, being throaty in sound, and so can never take a dagheš. An easy way of remembering the function of dagheš forte is to recall that in music the expression "forte forte" is shortened to "ff", *i.e.*, the single letter is doubled.

When dagheš forte is found in the bᵉghadhkᵉphath letters, the doubled sound is of course hard. Thus כִּפֵּר is "kĭppēr" and not "kĭphphēr". There can never be any actual confusion between dagheš forte and dagheš lene, since the former is always preceded by a vowel whilst the latter never is.

Certain letters when written with a šᵉwa frequently omit dagheš forte. These consonants are מ נ ק י ל ו (pointed מִנְקִילוּ mĭnqîlû, for easy memorising). Examples of this are וַיְהִי (wăyᵉhî), not וַיְּהִי (wăyyᵉhî), and הַלֲלוּ (hălᵃlû), not הַלְּלוּ (hăllᵃlû).

Dagheš forte is commonly employed as a characteristic mark of certain grammatical forms; for example, in the "intensive" form of the regular verb we would write קִטֵּל rather than קִטֵל or קְטַטֵל. Occasionally a dagheš is inserted in a consonant to give greater strength to the preceding vowel, as in לָמָּה (lāmâ), and less frequently in a consonant which has a vocal šᵉwa, to ensure its more audible enunciation, e.g., עִקְּבוֹת for עִקְבוֹת ('ĭqqᵉbhôth). This latter is called "dagheš forte dirimens" by some scholars and "dagheš forte disjunctive" by others.

Exercise 4

(a) Correct the following words:

1. בְּנֵי 2. יִשְׂכְּלוּ 3. קֶרֶב 4. שָׂרִים 5. יָדְעְתַּי 6. נָדוֹל

7. אָדָם 8. כִּבַּדְתָּ 9. בָּתוֹד 10. כָּלְפָם.

(b) Write in Hebrew:

1. hăllê.　　2. mĕlqᵉkhăth.　　3. mĕkhĕbh.　　4. šĭggēr.
5. mălkᵉkhû.　　6. bᵉkhĕm.　　7. lăʻᵃrăth.　　8. yĭbbām.
9. mĭdhbᵉrû.　　10. kĭppēnî.

CHAPTER V

THE GUTTURAL AND QUIESCENT LETTERS

WE have already observed that the letters א ה ח ע are styled "guttural," and to these may now be added the letter ר, which in certain respects may be regarded as coming within the same class. Their special characteristics are as follows :

None of these letters can take dagheš forte, and when the dagheš ought to be present, a short vowel preceding it is lengthened in compensation. For example, whereas a certain form of the regular verb קָטַל (qāṭǎl) is קִטֵּל (qǐṭṭēl), the corresponding form of בָּרַךְ (bārǎkh) is not בִּרֵּךְ (bǐrrēkh) but בֵּרֵךְ (bērēkh), the hireq being lengthened to çere, since ר cannot be doubled. This procedure always happens before א and ר, and frequently before ע. With ה and ח, on the other hand, the compensatory lengthening is seldom needed, since their sounds are by nature almost as strong as a normally reduplicated consonant. In such cases the guttural is said to have an "implicit" dagheš, i.e., not הָהוּא (hāhû') but הַהוּא (hǎhû'), and is given the Latin name of "dagheš forte implicitum".

Gutturals never take a simple vocal šᵉwa, but always an augmented one, and often prefer a compound šᵉwa to a simple silent one. So we would write

אֱלֹהִים ('elōhîm) rather than אֶלֹהִים, and יַחֲזִיק (yăḥᵃzîq) in place of יַחְזִיק. Whilst, as we have already noticed, א prefers an "e" vowel (seghol or hateph seghol), the other gutturals generally have pathah under or preceding them. Thus, whilst we would write מֶלֶךְ (mĕlĕkh) with seghol, the word מֶלַח (mĕlăḥ), ending in a guttural, takes pathah. Hireq under gutturals, however, is rare. Any short vowel occurring before a final guttural except א becomes pathah. If a guttural is preceded by a short vowel, the šᵉwa resulting under the guttural is the short-vowel augment of the hateph, e.g., בַּעֲלִי (bă‘ᵃlî), יֶאֱמֹר (yĕ'ᵉmôr), לְחָעֳלִי (lŏḥᵒlî).

In practice we shall see that when a final guttural letter is preceded by any long vowel except qameç, it is not easy to articulate, and this difficulty was overcome by slipping in a pathah sound between the long vowel and the final guttural. The pathah in such a case is written under the guttural but is pronounced before it, e.g., רוּחַ is pronounced "rûăḥ" instead of being רוּח (rûḥ). This device is called "pathah furtive". When a word of this sort no longer terminates in a guttural the pathah disappears, e.g., רוּחִי (rûḥî).

Exercise 5

Correct and pronounce the following words:

1. לְאֱמֶת 2. חֲכָמִים 3. שָׂרִים 4. מִשְׁחֲדוּ 5. רוּחוּ 6. הֵיֵלֵךְ

7. מֵאָדָם 8. זָבַח 9. בַּעֲלִי 10. לְעֲבִיר.

The Quiescent Letters are א ה ו י, and they frequently surrender their ordinary consonantal function in favour of coalescing or uniting with surrounding vowel sounds, and thus becoming silent or "quiescent". This, however, may happen only at the end of a syllable or word. When they occur at the beginning they are treated as full consonants. Final א is always silent, whilst yodh and waw are only silent when accompanied by a homogeneous vowel. The latter two consonants coalesce to form full hireq and çere, and full holem and šureq respectively, *i.e.*, ִ ; ֵ ; וֹ ; וּ. Thus עֵינֵי is "'ênê", not "'êynêy", and הוּא is "hû'", not "hûw'". But when any other sort of vowel than those which are homogeneous to them, as above, is introduced, they retain their consonantal pronunciation. Thus הַו is "hăw" and גּוֹ is "gôy". Sometimes the consonants yodh and waw combine with vowels to produce sounds analogous to our diphthongs, as follows :

ַי or ָי is pronounced ai as in aisle, *e.g.*, סוּסַי (sûsāy).

וֹי is pronounced oi as in toil, *e.g.*, הוֹי (hôy).

ָיו is pronounced ou as in foul, *e.g.*, סוּסָיו (sûsâw).

When these consonants quiesce, they do not take the silent šewa, *e.g.*, יֹאמֵר (yō'mēr), not יׂאְמֵר. When quiescent letters occur between a vowel and a

strongly enunciated consonant, they are not pronounced, *e.g.*, רֹאשׁ (rô'š). Where a quiescent letter
terminates a word, the final vowel is generally long,
since otherwise the syllable would be virtually left
open, *e.g.*, מָצָא (māçā') for מְצָא.

CHAPTER VI

PRELIMINARY MARKS AND ACCENTS

SOME notice may now be taken of certain accents and their function in relation to words and sentences.

Măppîq (מַפִּיק, "extending") is the name given to the dagheš inserted in a final ה to ensure its pronunciation as a full consonant. Thus, whilst מָה would be "mâ", דָּמָה is "dāmāh", with the ה audibly enunciated. Similarly, גָּבַה is "gābhăh".

Rāphĕ (רָפֶה "soft") is a short horizontal line written above the letter to call attention to the absence or omission of a dagheš forte or mappiq in the interests of smoother enunciation, e.g., וּלְמְקַצֵּה (ûlᵉmĭqçēh) for וּלְמְקַצֵּה.

Măqqēph (מַקֵּף, "binding"), is a small horizontal stroke written at the top of the line, between two or more words, to connect them in such a way that they become one for purposes of tonal stress and accentuation. Thus, whereas the words כֹּל (kōl) and אָדָם ('ādhăm) would each have their own accents, when joined by maqqeph the accent for the phrase thus formed becomes milra', i.e., כָּל־אָדָם, and because of this the holem of כֹּל becomes the short vowel qameç hatuph, since it is now in a shut unaccented syllable. The same happens with the accusative particle אֵת, which, when joined to another word, loses its own accentuation and thus has a short vowel, e.g., אֶת־כָּל־עֵשֶׂב ('ĕth-kŏl-'ēsĕbh). When זֶה (zĕh) and מָה (mâ) are joined to the next word by maqqeph, a "conjunctive" daghèš forte is always inserted in the initial letter following maqqeph, e.g., זֶה־סוּסִי (zĕh-ṣûṣî) or מַה־לָּךְ (măh-lāk).

Mĕthĕg (מֶתֶג "bridle") is a small perpendicular stroke placed to the left of a vowel in close proximity to the tone, to make sure that the vowel is properly pronounced and not neglected in favour of accenting the tone vowel. Metheg is placed by the second full open syllable from the tone, whether it is long, e.g., הָאָדָם (hā-'ā-dhām), or short, e.g., הֶהָרִים (hĕ-hā-rîm). Metheg also stands by the vowel which precedes a simple or augmented šᵉwa, e.g., קָטְלָה (qāṭᵉlâ), פָּעֳלוֹ (pŏ'ᵒlô), and thus indicates that the šᵉwa is vocal. Again, this helps to distinguish between long "a" and short "o", as in אָכְלָה ('ŏkhlâ) and אָכְלָה ('ākhᵉlâ). In the latter word the šᵉwa with its consonant does duty as a syllable.

Hebrew, as we have noted, is a strongly accented language, and the purpose of the accent-symbols is generally twofold. Firstly, they show the relation of the particular word to the rest of the sentence by acting as punctuation marks, and secondly they serve to mark the tone syllable. For our present purposes only two major punctuation marks need be mentioned, as follows :

The sign (ְ) or 'Āthnāḥ (אַתְנָח) is placed under the tone syllable of the word which constitutes the most important logical pause within the sentence, which in English would probably be marked by a colon or semicolon.

Ṣillûq (סִלּיק) is a perpendicular line identical in form with metheg, and is always placed under the tone syllable of the last word of a verse, which is then always followed by the Hebrew "period" or "full stop" (:), the Ṣôph pāṣûq (סוֹף פָּסוּק), e.g.,: הָאָרֶץ.

Though the same sign does duty for metheg and silluq, and though they can both occur in the same word, e.g., מֵהָאָדָם (mēhā'ādhām), there need be no real confusion. If the perpendicular stroke comes under the accented syllable at the end of a verse it must be silluq ; if it is found under a word in the middle of a verse it is metheg. If it is under the tone it is silluq ; if it is under the second full syllable from the tone and that syllable is open, it is metheg.

A word is said to be "in pause" when it has 'athnah or silluq as its accentuation, and any short vowel thus accented becomes long. Thus, מַיִם (măyĭm) in pause becomes: מָיִם with silluq or מָיִם with 'athnah. Most sentences in the Hebrew Bible

will be seen to illustrate the position of these two
major stops.

When perusing a Hebrew Bible the reader will
notice in the margin at the bottom of the page a
number of variant readings, consisting of consonants
which are to be preferred to their counterparts in the
text. Because the ancient Hebrew text was regarded
as sacred, the consonants therein could not be
modified or disturbed at all, hence the variants were
assigned to the foot of the page in the printed text.
The original consonantal text was called the Kᵉthîbh
(כְּתִיב, "written"), whilst the variants were named
Qᵉrê (קְרֵי "to be read"). Generally an asterisk or
small circle calls attention in the text to the presence
of a variant. The procedure then is to read the
consonants of the Qᵉre in conjunction with the
vowels already under the particular word in the
Kᵉthibh. Thus, in Psalm ix. 13, the Kᵉthibh is
עֲנִיִּם whilst the marginal consonantal variant reads
עניים קרי, i.e., "עניים is to be read". Thus the
correct word combines the vowels of the Kᵉthibh
with the consonants of the Qᵉre, which is עֲנָוִים.

In instances of such frequent occurrence that it
would be tedious to print the Qᵉre each time the
Kᵉthibh requires such modification, a permanent
Qᵉre or "Qᵉre perpetuum" has been devised, which
the student retains in his memory. In this, the

vowels for the variant reading are placed in the text
as usual, but the consonants are omitted from the
margin, and the reader substitutes the reading for
the Kᵉthibh without being warned to do so by an
asterisk or circle appearing over the word in question.

The Divine Name illustrates this adequately.
יהוה, the name of the God of Israel, is generally
pointed יְהוָה, from which by transliteration comes
our hybrid English form "Jehovah". It was
regarded as too sacred to pronounce in its original
form (which may have sounded something like
"Yahweh"), so another sound was supplied by the
word אֲדֹנָי ('adhonāy), and the consonants יהוה were
given the pointing of אֲדֹנָי, making the impossible
form יְהוָֹה (the hateph under א becoming a simple
šᵉwa under י).

The consonantal form of the third singular personal pronoun "she" appears frequently in the
Pentateuch as הִוא. At some time confusion has
arisen between the masculine הוא (hû') and the
feminine הִיא (hî'), and this is obvious from the
Kᵉthibh (הִוא). Again, the Qᵉre for the feminine is
not given because it occurs so often.

CHAPTER VII

THE DEFINITE ARTICLE

THERE is no indefinite article in Hebrew. Thus מַיִם
(mǎyĭm) means "water" or "waters", and יוֹם (yôm)
means "a day", representing the noun in its simplest
form. When we wish to say "the waters" or "the
day", it is necessary to employ a prefix, the consonant ה, with various vowels accompanying it.
Originally the definite article may have been הַל (like
the Arabic article "al" as in "algebra"), with the ל
being assimilated to the next consonant, and this
may be the reason why daghes forte is used frequently
with the article.

Generally the article is ה, pointed with pathah and
followed by daghes forte in the first consonant of the
word to which it is prefixed. When such a word
begins with א ה ח ע or ר, the daghes forte cannot be
inserted, since these letters are guttural in force, and
the pathah of the article in such cases is lengthened
to qameç in compensation, except with ה and ח.
When ע and ה as initial letters have the tone or
accent, and are written with qameç, the pointing of
the article is again qameç, but when they occur
with qameç and do not take the tone, the pointing
of the article then becomes sᵉghol. Before חָ and הָ
the article always takes sᵉghol.

These rules may be conveniently illustrated in tabular form as follows :

Before Consonants	Article Pointing	Examples
Ordinary	הַ	הַקּוֹל, הַמַּיִם
א ע ר	הָ	הָאוֹר, הָעַיִן, הָראֹשׁ.
ה ח	הַ	הַהוּא, הַחֹשֶׁךְ
עֲ הֳ	הָ	הָעָם, הָהָר
עָ הָ	הֶ	הֶעָפָר, הֶהָרִים
חָ חֲ	הֶ	הֶחָכָם, הֶחֳלִי

In a few common nouns the vowel of the initial consonant is lengthened to qameç when the article is prefixed. These words include אֶרֶץ (’ĕrĕç), הַר (hăr), עַם (’ăm), and רַע (ră‘), which become הָאָרֶץ (hā’ārĕç), הָהָר (hāhār), הָעָם (hā‘ām) and הָרָע (hārā‘).

The article in Hebrew may be used demonstratively, *e.g.*, הַיּוֹם means "this day" or "to-day". The vocative is also expressed by the article on occasions, as הַבַּעַל "O Baal", and is sometimes used generically to designate the member of a class where English usage would lead us to expect an indefinite article, *e.g.,* "an enemy" in Hebrew is הָאֹיֵב (hā'ōyēbh). The article is also attached to an attributive adjective qualifying a definite noun. So "the good man" would be "the man, the good one". A further distinctive use of the article is with proper names, to show that the individual is supreme in his class, *e.g.,* "God" is הָאֱלֹהִים (hā'elōhîm).

From this point we shall abandon the practice of transliterating each Hebrew word, except in special cases where the modification of the word affects the pronunciation, and which would not be recognisable by other means. We shall also introduce a vocabulary before each subsequent exercise, which the student is expected to learn carefully. In these vocabularies all nouns will be considered to be masculine unless otherwise marked.

VOCABULARY

אֶרֶץ	earth (*f*).	שָׁמַיִם	heavens.	טוֹב	good.
יוֹם	day.	עַם	people.	רַע	bad.
אִישׁ	man.	אֱלֹהִים	God (*pl.*).	עַיִן	eye (*f*).
קוֹל	voice.	בֹּקֶר	morning.	עָפָר	dust.
מֶלֶךְ	king.	מַיִם	water(s) (*pl.*)	רָקִיעַ	firmament.
אִשָּׁה	woman (*f*).	עִיר	city (*f*).	גָּדוֹל	great.
רָם	high.	חֹשֶׁךְ	darkness.	אוֹר	light.

Exercise 6

Write out the following :

The man, the people, the waters, to-day, the king, the firmament, the voice, the darkness, the eye, the morning, a woman, a day, the dust, the light.

CHAPTER VIII

THE CONJUNCTION : ADJECTIVES

THE usual form of the conjunction "and" in Hebrew is waw with simple vocal šᵉwa, but there are variations of this as follows :

Under ordinary circumstances it is וְ, e.g., אִישׁ וְאִשָּׁה, (man and woman.) Because it is a labial it cannot have a šᵉwa before another labial sound, and so it becomes וּ before מ ו ב and פ, e.g., וּפָרָה, (and a cow). This is the only exception to the rule which we learned earlier, that no Hebrew word begins with a vowel, but even here the consonantal waw, in one sense, still begins the spelling of the word, and only becomes a vowel (šureq) by the addition of dagheš in its bosom.

If the conjunction comes immediately before the accent, however, the waw may have qameç instead of being šureq, e.g., לֶחֶם וָמַיִם, bread and water. Before another šᵉwa it also becomes šureq, e.g., וּדְבָרִים, (and words), but before a hateph it takes the corresponding short vowel, שׁוֹר וַחֲמוֹר, ox and ass.

When occurring before yodh with šᵉwa, the yodh quiesces and the conjunction then takes hireq, e.g., וִיהוּדָה and Judah, not וְיְהוּדָה. Before יהוה the con-

junction takes pathah, *i.e.*, וַיְהִי, but when written
to אֱלֹהִים it takes çere, which is then assimilated into
the vowel sound under the 'aleph to become וַאלֹהִים,
and God, for וֵאלֹהִים.   When a word is written with
the article, the conjunction does not displace the ה of
the article, *e.g.*, וְהָאִישׁ, and the man.

Adjectives

When an adjective qualifies a noun in Hebrew, it
follows it in the order of words.   Thus, "a good man"
would be "a man, a good one", *i.e.*, אִישׁ טוֹב.   The
adjective always agrees in gender and number with
its noun, as in other languages.   Until we have
learned the inflections of the noun we will confine
ourselves to the masculine singular form as above.
When the adjective is used predicatively, *e.g.*, "the
man is good", it does not take the article and
generally precedes the noun.

The present tense of the verb "to be" is not
normally expressed in Hebrew.   Thus the sentence
"the man is good" would be rendered "the man (is)
good" (הָאִישׁ טוֹב), or more frequently "good (is) the
man" (טוֹב הָאִישׁ).   When an attributive adjective
qualifies a definite noun, it has the article attached.
So, "the good man" would be הָאִישׁ הַטּוֹב, *i.e.*, "the
man, the good one".   If there is more than one
adjective, the article is repeated with each, *e.g.*, "the
great and good day" becomes הַיּוֹם הַגָּדוֹל וְהַטּוֹב.

VOCABULARY

הַר	mountain.	זָהָב	gold.	כֶּסֶף	silver.
רֹאשׁ	head.	קָצֵר	short.	יָד	hand (*f*).
דָּבָר	word.	אֶבֶן	stone (*f*).	בַּת	daughter (*f*).
עֶרֶב	evening.	חֳלִי	disease.	נָבִיא	prophet.
לַיְלָה	night.	הֵיכָל	temple, palace.	חֶרֶב	sword (*f*).
יַרְכָה	side (*f*).	קָרָא	to call.	רָאָה	to see.

Exercise 7

Translate the following :

‏(a) 1. טוֹב הַנָּבִיא   2. הַנָּבִיא הַטּוֹב   3. הַבֹּקֶר הַגָּדוֹל וְהַטּוֹב
‏4. רָם הָהָר   5. הָאִישׁ וְהַנָּבִיא   6. הַהֵיכָל נָּדוֹל וְטוֹב
‏7. הַלַּיְלָה וְהַיּוֹם 8. הַבַּת וְהָאִשָּׁה 9. הָאִישׁ הַמֶּלֶךְ 10. טוֹב
‏הַזָּהָב.

(*b*) 1. The great man. 2. To-day. 3. The evening and
the morning. 4. Gold and silver. 5. The king is great
and good. 6. The hand and the eye. 7. The woman
and the man. 8. The people is great. 9. The disease
and the prophet. 10. The great day and the bad night.

CHAPTER IX

THE NOUN AND ITS INFLECTION

THERE are only two genders in Hebrew, masculine and feminine, and three numbers, singular, plural and dual. The dual is used with nouns only, chiefly with objects coming in pairs.

The masculine nouns in the singular have scarcely any termination to indicate their gender, whereas in the feminine there are several distinctive terminations.

Masculine nouns may be classified thus :

(a) Names of members of the male sex, with their office, *e.g..*, דָּוִד David, סוּס horse, שֹׁפֵט judge.

(b) Names of kingdoms and peoples, *e.g.*, אַשּׁוּר, people of Assyria, יִשְׂרָאֵל, Israel.

(c) Names of mountains, rivers, metals ; months of the year, *e.g.*, לְבָנוֹן Lebanon, פְּרָת Euphrates, כֶּסֶף silver, אָבִיב Abib.

The plural ending of masculine nouns is ◌ִים, or written defectively, ◌ִם, and is generally attached to the singular form, *e.g.*, סוּסִים, horses. The ending ◌ֶה modifies to ◌ִים in plural forms, *e.g.*, רֹעֶה becomes רֹעִים, shepherds. Not all masculine nouns have the normal plural ending, however ; אָב

father, is אָבוֹת in the plural, whilst others have an irregular form, *e.g.*, אִישׁ in the plural is אֲנָשִׁים.

Nouns ending in הָ‑ are generally feminine, and this form was an original ‑תְ or ‑תָ, the former of which is preserved in some names, *e.g.*, אֵילַת Elath, נַחַת rest. A great number of forms are construed as feminine, however, which do not possess the feminine ending.

Feminine nouns may be classified as follows :

(*a*) Names of females, with their functions, *e.g.*, מִרְיָם Miriam, אֵם mother, כַּלָּה bride.

(*b*) Names of the elements, *e.g.*, אֵשׁ fire, אֶרֶץ earth, אֶבֶן stone.

(*c*) Countries regarded as mothers of their peoples : פָּרָס Persia, צִיּוֹן Zion.

(*d*) Organs of the body coming in pairs : יָד hand, רֶגֶל foot, קֶרֶן horn.

(*e*) Things abstract : נֶפֶשׁ soul, life, בְּכוֹרָה birthright, טוֹבָה goodness.

(*f*) Names of instruments and utensils : כּוֹס cup, חֶרֶב sword, מִשְׁכָּב couch.

The plural ending of feminine nouns is וֹת‑, or written defectively ת‑. When the singular form has no feminine ending, the plural termination is joined immediately to it, *e.g.*, בְּאֵר well, בְּאֵרוֹת. The ordinary feminine singular ending is replaced by the plural termination, *e.g.*, שָׂרָה princess, becomes שָׂרוֹת princesses.

The above inflections may be clarified by means of a table :

Masculine Singular	Feminine Singular	Masculine Plural	Feminine Plural
סוּס	סוּסָה	סוּסִים	סוּסוֹת
נָבִיא	נְבִיאָה	נְבִיאִים	נְבִיאוֹת
דָּג	דָּגָה	דָּגִים	דָּגוֹת

The dual masculine and feminine of סוּס would be סוּסַיִם and סוּסָתַיִם respectively.

The dual ending ־ַיִם used above is found with both masculine and feminine nouns. It is employed for substantives and pairs of objects as follows :

(*a*) Bodily organs : אָזְנַיִם ears, רַגְלַיִם two feet.

(*b*) Objects comprising two parts : מֶלְקָחַיִם tongs, דְּלָתַיִם double-door.

(*c*) Double and quantitative numbers : שְׁנַיִם two, שִׁבְעָתַיִם sevenfold.

Adjectives, as we have seen, agree in gender and number with the nouns which they qualify, *e.g.*, the good woman, הָאִשָׁה הַטוֹבָה, good years, שָׁנִים טוֹבוֹת.

Some nouns are found only in plural form, the most common being שָׁמַיִם heaven, מַיִם water, פָּנִים face, חַיִּים life, עֲלוּמִים youth, זְקֻנִים old age.

Some common nouns of masculine gender with the plural form in ־וֹת are:

אָב	father.	מִזְבֵּחַ	altar.	עוֹר	skin.
חֲלוֹם	dream.	מָקוֹם	place.	קוֹל	voice.
לֵב, לֵבָב	heart.	בְּאֵר	well, cistern.	שֻׁלְחָן	table.
לַיְלָה	night.	אוֹת	sign.	שֵׁם	name.
שׁוֹפָר	trumpet.	מַקֵּל	staff.	כִּסֵּא	throne.

Some common feminine nouns with the plural form in ־ִים are:

אֶבֶן	stone.	עִיר	city.	שְׂעוֹרָה	barley.
אִשָּׁה	woman.	חִטָּה	wheat.	מִלָּה	word.
יוֹנָה	dove.	אֵלָה	terebinth.	תְּאֵנָה	fig tree.

VOCABULARY

אֹזֶן	ear (f).	כּוֹכָב	star.	רֶגֶל	foot (f).
פַּר	ox.	מִדְבָּר	desert.	נַעַל	sandal (f).
שָׁמַע	to hear.	עֵץ	tree.	דָּג	fish.
יֶלֶד	boy.	שָׂפָה	lip (f).	לָקַח	to take.
עַל־	over, upon	קָדוֹשׁ	holy.	יָשַׁב	to sit.
אֶל־	unto.	צַדִּיק	righteous.	שַׁבָּת	sabbath.
אֵשׁ	fire.	קֶרֶן	horn (f).	הֲלֹם	hither.

Exercise 8

(*a*) Translate :

‏5. הַיַּרְכָתַיִם 4. הַיָּדַיִם 3. אָבוֹת 2. סוּסִים 1. דְּבָרִים
‏10. רַגְלַיִם 9. עָרִים 8. בְּאֵרוֹת 7. לְבָבוֹת 6. זְקֵנִים

(*b*) 1. Tables. 2. Stones. 3. Two-years. 4. Trumpets.
5. The horse and the mare. 6. Good fathers. 7. The
princess is great. 8. Two eyes and two ears. 9. Good
men and good women. 10. Sons and daughters.

CHAPTER X

PRONOUNS AND PARTICLES

PRONOUNS do duty for nouns, and may be separable or inseparable. The Personal pronoun is used only to express the nominative case, but in fragmentary form it is attached to other words to represent the oblique cases.

The Personal pronoun is as follows :

Singular	Plural
אֲנִי I אָנֹכִי I	אֲנַחְנוּ we.
אַתָּה thou (*m.*)	אַתֶּם you (*m.*)
אַתְּ thou (*f.*)	אַתֵּן, אַתֵּנָה you (*f.*)
הוּא he	הֵם, הֵמָּה they (*m.*)
הִיא she	(הֵן) הֵנָּה they (*f.*)

Modifications occur in pause, *e.g.*, first singular אָנִי, אָנֹכִי, second singular masculine אָתָּה, second singular feminine אָתְּ, first plural אֲנַחְנוּ. Both second plural feminine forms are rare.

The third person of the pronoun is sometimes used

as a copulative in the appropriate gender and number in sentences where the verb "to be" occurs :

The woman is good. הָאִשָּׁה הִיא טוֹבָה

The mountains are lofty. הֶהָרִים הֵם רָמִים

Jehovah is (the) God. יהוה הוּא הָאֱלֹהִים

Sometimes the third person pronoun is used with a subject of the second person, *e.g.*, Thou (he) art the God, אַתָּה הוּא הָאֱלֹהִים.

Demonstrative Pronouns

The pronouns used to indicate relative objects are :

	Masculine	Feminine
this	זֶה	זֹאת
these	אֵלֶּה	אֵלֶּה
that	הוּא	הִיא
those	הֵם, הֵמָּה	(הֵן) הֵנָּה

When a demonstrative is used adjectivally it follows the noun, which is definite, and so it too takes the article, *e.g.*, "that day" becomes הַיּוֹם הַהוּא. When used predicatively they do not take the article, and the order of the Hebrew follows that of the English. So "this is the good man" is זֶה הָאִישׁ הַטּוֹב. The demonstrative of the near object when repeated acquires a correlative significance, "the one . . . the other" (זֶה . . . זֶה or זֹאת . . . זֹאת) ; and "some . . . others" (אֵלֶּה . . . אֵלֶּה).

Interrogative Pronoun

The absence of a question mark in Hebrew makes it necessary for simple questions to have some characteristic interrogative prefix. One of these is the particle ה, which is pointed as follows :

(a) With ordinary consonants it is הֲ, e.g., הֲזֶה is this ?

(b) With simple šᵉwa as the first vowel it is הַ, e.g., הַמְאֹד, is it much ? This is sometimes followed by dagheš forte.

(c) Before gutturals without qameç it is הַ, e.g., הַאַתָּה art thou ?

(d) Before any guttural with qameç the ה takes sᵉghol, e.g., הֶחָזָק is it strong ?

Two other interrogative pronouns are also used : מִי "who ?" which is invariable in form, and מָה "what ?" Both of these are indeclinable, and usually come first in a sentence. The pointing of מָה is exactly like that of the article, and it is joined by maqqeph to the next word, with the insertion of dagheš forte in non-guttural letters, e.g., מַה־זֶּה what is this ?, מָה־אָנִי what am I ?

מָה may also be used as an exclamatory expression with another word, *e.g.*, מַה־נּוֹרָא הַמָּקוֹם הַזֶּה, how dreadful is this place ! (Genesis xxviii. 17). Before verbs and adverbs it frequently does duty as an adverb, *e.g.*, מַה־טּוֹב how good. מִי and מָה may be used in an indefinite sense to mean "whoever" and "whatever".

Relative Pronouns

The word אֲשֶׁר is indeclinable and is a general term of relation which is made specific by some other word in the context. Thus whilst we would say in English, "the house where he dwelt" (שָׁכַן), the Hebrew idiom would render it "the house which he dwelt there", the last word of the phrase defining the exact nature of the relation, *i.e.*, הַבַּיִת אֲשֶׁר שָׁכַן שָׁם. Similarly, "the house whence he came (בָּא)" would be הַבַּיִת אֲשֶׁר בָּא מִשָּׁם, *i.e.*, "the house that he came from there".

Notice should be taken of the following combinations :

שָׁם there,	שָׁם . . . אֲשֶׁר where.	
שָׁמָּה thither,	שָׁמָּה . . . אֲשֶׁר whither.	
מִשָּׁם thence,	מִשָּׁם . . . אֲשֶׁר whence.	

Other pronominal expressions are :

שָׁם . . . פֹּה	here . . there.
לֹא . . . אִישׁ	nobody ("not a man").

כָּל . . . לֹא
or
לֹא . . . כָּל   none ("not any").

אִישׁ . . . אִישׁ   one . . . another.

אֵלֶּה . . . אֵלֶּה   some . . . others.

VOCABULARY

עָשָׂה	to do.	תּוֹרָה	law (f).	גִּבּוֹר	mighty man,
שֶׁמֶשׁ	sun.	פֶּה	mouth.		hero.
נֶפֶשׁ	soul (f).	נָתַן	to give, set.	שִׁיר	song.
בַּיִת	house.	זָכַר	to remember.	רוּחַ	wind,
בֵּן	son.	שָׁכַח	to forget.		spirit (f).
יָרַד	to go down.	דָּם	blood.	שָׁמַר	to keep.
סוּס	horse.	אָסַף	to gather.	יָם	sea.
מִצְוָה	command (f).	לֹא	not.	מַלְכָּה	queen (f).
אֲהָהּ	alas !	בְּרָכָה	blessing.	דֶּרֶךְ	way.

Exercise 9

Translate :

1. אֲנִי הָאִישׁ. 2. הַחֹשֶׁךְ הַגָּדוֹל הוּא הַלַּיְלָה. 3. אַתְּ הַבַּת
הַטּוֹבָה. 4. הוּא אִישׁ טוֹב. 5. מַה־הִיא. 6. הַגִּבּוֹרִים הָאֵלֶּה
7. מַה־זֹּאת אֲשֶׁר עָשָׂה. 8. הַבַּת הַטּוֹבָה הַהִיא. 9. מָה־רָם
הַמָּקוֹם הַזֶּה. 10. הֶעָצוּם מְאֹד הוּא.

1. These are the wise men. 2. Those heavens. 3. This
woman is good. 4. This good man. 5. This is the good and
powerful man. 6. What a city ! 7. What a palace !
8. He is the man who was over the house. 9. I am the
powerful king who is over the great land. 10. These are
the heavens and the earth and the sea.

CHAPTER XI

THE INSEPARABLE PREPOSITIONS

ORIGINALLY the prepositions with which we are now concerned were nouns, but have become fragmentary in process of time and are always prefixed to the word which they govern. They are :

בְּ, in, on, by, with (perhaps from an original בַּיִת).

כְּ, like, about, as, according to (from a possible original כֵּן).

לְ, at, to, for (perhaps from אֶל־ or אַל־).

The rules for pointing are as follows :

(a) The general pointing is šᵉwa, e.g., בְּעִיר in a city כְּאֶבֶן like a stone.

(b) Before another šᵉwa they take hireq in the ordinary way, e.g., לִבְרָכָה,, for a blessing, not לְבְרָכָה.

(c) Before gutturals with a hateph the šᵉwa is replaced by the corresponding short vowel of the augment, e.g., כַּאֲרִי like a lion. The only exceptions to this are words like אֱלֹהִים which are frequently found in the text, where the א becomes quiescent, the hateph sᵉghol is removed, and the preposition takes çere, i.e., לֵאלֹהִים. The Divine Name יהוה, taking its pointing from אֲדוֹנָי, has pathah under the preposition in the same way, e.g., לַאדוֹנָי for לַאֲדוֹנָי, and so לַיהוָה.

(d) If the preposition falls in the pretone, the vowel under it is frequently qameç, e.g., בְּמַיִם in water, לְבֶטַח securely.

(e) A word which has the article prefixed also generally surrenders the ה, and the preposition then assumes its vowel, e.g., לְהָאִישׁ to the man, becomes לָאִישׁ ; בְּהַסֵּפֶר becomes בַּסֵּפֶר.

The preposition לְ frequently indicates a dative of possession, as in the phrase "the man has a daughter", which becomes בַּת לָאִישׁ, "there is a daughter to the man". The inseparable prepositions are frequently joined with מה to form adverbs, thus לָמָה why? ; בַּמֶּה or בַּמָּה, wherein? ; כַּמֶּה, כַּמָּה, how much? ; עַד־מֶה, עַד־מָה, how long? ; עַל־מֶה, עַל־מָה, wherefore, whereupon.

The preposition מִן is partly separable and partly not. When followed by the article it may remain separable, and is followed by maqqeph, e.g., מִן־הָעִיר, from the city, though the final ן may be dropped and the hireq lengthened to çere as a compensation, e.g., מֵהָעִיר. מִן does not displace the consonant of the article like the inseparable prepositions.

Before non-gutturals the weak terminal ן is generally assimilated to the following consonant, which being in effect doubled takes a compensative dagheš forte, e.g., מִמֶּלֶךְ from a king, instead of מִנְמֶלֶךְ. The dagheš may be omitted from a letter pointed with šᵉwa, *e.g.*, מְמְלִילוֹת for מִמְּלִילוֹת. When the initial consonant is yodh with šᵉwa, the dagheš is omitted whilst the yodh drops the šᵉwa and coalesces to form long hireq, *e.g.*, מִירִיחוֹ, from Jericho, for מִיְרִיחוֹ. Before gutturals or ר the full form may be used, מִן־עִיר from a city, or the final ן may be dropped and the hireq lengthened to çere, *e.g.*, מֵעֵץ, from a tree, for מִן־עֵץ, making the preposition inseparable.

VOCABULARY

אֲרִי	lion.	בְּהֵמָה	beast,	בְּרִית	covenant.
חֲמוֹר	ass.		cattle. (*f*)		(*f*).
מְאֹד	very.	שָׁבַת	to rest.	עַד־עוֹלָם	for ever.
אָדָם	mankind.	שָׁפַךְ	to shed.	מָשַׁל (בְּ)	to rule
אֲדָמָה	ground (*f*).	שָׁאַל	to ask.		(over).
כָּתַב	to write.	תְּפִלָּה	prayer (*f*).	פָּעַל	to do.
כָּרַת	to cut.	עַד־	until, unto.	שְׁמוּאֵל	Samuel.
יְהוֹשֻׁעַ	Joshua.	רַב	much	יוֹסֵף	Joseph.
מִצְרַיִם	Egypt.	(*pl.* רַבִּים).		אָח	brother.
עוֹלָם	age,	אֹכֶל	food.	חָדַל	to leave
	duration.	מֵעוֹלָם	from of old.		off, cease.

Exercise 10

Translate:

1. בְּשָׁלוֹם. 2. כַּיהוָֹה. 3. לְחָלִי. 4. לִשְׁמוּאֵל. 5. יוֹם וָלַיְלָה

הֵם בַּשָּׁמַיִם. 6. בֵּן לַמֶּלֶךְ. 7. לֶחֶם וָמַיִם הֵם טוֹבִים מְאֹד

8. מַחֲשֵׁךְ עַד־הַיּוֹם. 9. עָפָר מִן־הָאֲדָמָה אֲנַחְנוּ. 10. הָאֱלֹהִים

הוּא בַּהֵיכָל הַזֶּה.

1. In God.   2. As a lion.   3. To Joshua.   4. Jehovah is in the heavens.   5. From the mountain.   6. The son is like the king.   7. On the lofty mountain in the morning. 8. The palace is for the king.   9. The wise people are in the temple in the evening.   10. The prophet has a daughter and a son.

CHAPTER XII

THE VERB: ORDER OF WORDS

In earlier chapters we have considered two important groups of words which comprise the sentence, namely nouns and particles, and on this basis we have been able to build up small synthetic Hebrew sentences. Now we have to begin consideration of an important component of all sentences, and that is the verb. In Hebrew there are a number of inflections and tenses which express developed meanings of the simple verb stem, but we shall leave the bulk of these to later sections, and concentrate on the parts necessary for simple expression.

The verb generally stands first in order at the beginning of a sentence, and elsewhere precedes its subject. This structure emphasises the importance of the verb as the "action-word" of the sentence. The presence of a direct object of a verb is indicated by means of a particle, אֵת, which is the sign of the accusative case, and is regularly used in prose before the direct object. If a noun is indefinite, or if it is the indirect object of a verb, the particle is not employed, nor is it used very much in poetic writings. אֵת is largely joined to its noun by maqqeph, and since it then becomes a shut syllable, the çere becomes s^eghol, *i.e.*, אֶת־. If there are more than one of such nouns, the accusative particle is repeated with each of them. Whereas in English and some other languages the root or simplest form of the verb is the infinitive, in Hebrew the third person singular of the perfect active is used instead. Thus, קָרָא does not really mean "to call", as is generally written in vocabularies and lexicons, but "he called".

The inflection of the verb is made by adding the endings of the personal pronoun to the root, observing the usual modifications in pointing with respect to the position of the tone. The verb קָטַל is used as a model for the paradigm, since it illustrates these inflections well, although it is a rare word found only in poetry. The perfect tense is as follows :

קָטַל	he killed, he has killed	(3rd sing. masc.)
קָטְלָה	she killed, has killed	(3rd sing. fem.)
קָטַלְתָּ	thou hast killed	(2nd sing. masc.)
קָטַלְתְּ	thou (f.) hast killed	(2nd sing. fem.)
קָטַלְתִּי	I killed, have killed	(1st sing. common)
קָטְלוּ	they killed, did kill	(3rd plur. common)
קְטַלְתֶּם	ye killed, have killed	(2nd plur. masc.)
קְטַלְתֶּן	ye (f) killed, have killed	(2nd plur. fem.)
קָטַלְנוּ	we killed, have killed	(1st plur. common)

To be strictly accurate we should speak of "forms" rather than "tenses" of the verb, since it is the completeness or otherwise of an action which is being expressed and not the time factor, as in English. Thus the perfect expresses completed action and

includes all perfect tenses such as future perfect and
pluperfect. The imperfect is concerned with un-
finished activity, and thus includes the future and
present alike. The various shades of the subjunctive
are also part of the category of the imperfect.

The inflection of the imperfect follows a similar
pattern to that of the perfect, as follows :

יִקְטֹל he will kill, may kill, was killing, etc.

(3rd sing. masc.)

תִּקְטֹל she will kill, may kill, was killing, etc.

(3rd sing. fem.)

תִּקְטֹל thou wilt kill, mayest kill, etc.

(2nd sing. masc.)

תִּקְטְלִי thou (*f.*) wilt kill, mayest kill, etc.

(2nd sing. fem.)

אֶקְטֹל I will kill, may kill, was killing, etc.

(1st sing. common)

יִקְטְלוּ they will kill, may kill, were killing, etc.

(3rd plur. masc.)

תִּקְטֹלְנָה they (*f.*) will kill, may kill, etc.

(3rd plur. fem.)

תִּקְטְלוּ ye will kill, may kill, were killing, etc.

(2nd plur. masc.)

תִּקְטֹלְנָה ye (*f.*) will kill, may kill, etc.

(2nd plur. fem.)

נִקְטֹל we will kill, may kill, were killing, etc.

(1st plur. common)

When the negative form of a verb is required, the

particle לֹא is used, and immediately precedes the verb. Thus the sentence "the man did not call the boy" would be לֹא קָרָא הָאִישׁ אֶת־הַיֶּלֶד.

VOCABULARY

שָׁכַן	to dwell.	נַעַר	lad.	הָלַךְ	to go.
בָּרָא	to create.	נַעֲרָה	girl (f).	הָרַג	to slay.
אָמַר	to say.	עוֹף	fowl.	אֹיֵב	enemy.
הָיָה	to be.	אָכַל	to eat.	הֵן, הִנֵּה	behold.
סֵפֶר	book.	שָׂרָף	seraph.	יִצְחָק	Isaac.
חָכָם	wise.	מָחָר	to-morrow.	מִדְבָּר	desert.
צָפוֹן	north.	עָצוּם	powerful.	מָחָה	to destroy.

Exercise 11

Translate :

1. שָׁמַעְתִּי אֶת־הַנָּבִיא 2. לֹא שָׁמְעָה הָאִשָּׁה אֶת־הַקּוֹל בַּן הַגָּדוֹל 3. זָכַרְתִּי אֵת הָאִישׁ אֲשֶׁר שָׁפַךְ אֶת־הַדָּם בַּמִּדְבָּר 4. כָּתַבְתִּי בַּסֵּפֶר בַּיּוֹם הַזֶּה 5. אֵלֶּה הַסּוּסוֹת הָרָעוֹת אֲשֶׁר הָרְגוּ בָּאֲדָמָה 6. יִשְׁמֹר אֵת הַמַּלְכָּה הַטּוֹבָה בַּהֵיכָל 7. וְהִנֵּה לָקַח הָאִישׁ אֶת־הָאִשָּׁה הַזֹּאת לְאִשָּׁה 8. וְהָאִישׁ יִצְחָק גָּדוֹל מְאֹד בָּאָרֶץ 9. תִּשְׁמְרוּ אֶת־הַמִּצְוֹת אֲשֶׁר נָתַן הָאֱלֹהִים 10. הָאִישׁ אֲשֶׁר בָּרָא הָאֱלֹהִים הוּא טוֹב.

1. I will write in a book. 2. Who are these mighty men and these prophets ? 3. One called to another and said, Great is Jehovah. 4. Thou (f) hast eaten from the tree. 5. Jehovah will hear the man who does not shed blood. 6. Did not God give a son and a daughter to the prophet ? 7. Ye (f) shall keep the words which are in the book. 8. God has created good and evil and day and night. 9. I remembered what I heard in the temple. 10. He will not keep the words which the prophet gave to the people in the desert.

CHAPTER XIII

THE CASES

CASE endings as such have not survived in Hebrew, any more than they have in modern Arabic. Indeed, it is difficult to think of cases at all in Hebrew in the strictest sense. At an earlier stage of the language there may have been three : nominative, accusative and genitive. The first of these has no distinctive indication, being recognisable either by its position in relation to the verb, or by the general sense of the passage in which it occurs.

The accusative is somewhat more clearly marked, since it frequently has the particle אֵת, which we discussed in the last chapter, and which is the usual sign of the accusative. A possible survival of an ancient accusative case-ending is seen in the un-accented הָ-, the so-called "hē locale", which generally indicates "motion towards", e.g., towards the north, is צָפֹנָה ; towards Babylon, is בָּבֶלָה.

The genitive relation has no case-endings, but is characterised by an intimate connection of nouns, and is known as the construct state. This may be illustrated by saying that, whereas in English we would say "the-word of-the-man," making "the word" absolute, and expressing "the man" in the

dependent genitive case, Hebrew reverses the process by recognising that "the word" would be
dependent upon "the man" for its expression.
Thus Hebrew would say "the-word-of the-man", or
more accurately "word-of the-man", thus putting
"word-of" in construction with the absolute "man".
Similarly, in the phrase "the horse of the king", the
noun in the absolute would be "king", whilst
"horse-of" would be in this dependent relation called
the construct state.

Whereas the absolute is never modified in its
form, the construct is shortened as much as the
language will allow, so as to be uttered quickly, with
the principal stress in pronunciation falling on the
absolute noun. As a result the construct has certain
modifications in form, which may be seen in the
masculine word דָּבָר thus :

absolute sing. דָּבָר (word) ; construct sing. דְּבַר
(word of).

absolute plur. דְּבָרִים (words) ; construct plur. דִּבְרֵי
(words of).

The construct singular shortens the absolute as
much as possible, whilst the construct plural elides
the terminal "m" of the absolute plural and changes
the full hireq to full çere. A feminine noun inflects
as follows :

absolute sing. סוּסָה (mare) ; construct sing. סוּסַת
(mare of).

absolute plur. סוּסוֹת (mares) ; construct plur. סוּסוֹת (mares of).

Whilst the feminine construct plural ends like the absolute, it must be shortened as much as possible. Thus the absolute plural of צְדָקָה, righteousness, is צְדָקוֹת but the construct is צִדְקוֹת, formed by rule from צְדָקוֹת. A dual construct from the absolute סוּסָתַיִם would be סוּסָתַי, the šᵉwa being vocal to represent an original full vowel.

A table of examples may assist in learning the modifications of the construct state :

	horse	mare	son	star	upright	queen
Ab. sing.	סוּס	סוּסָה	בֵּן	כּוֹכָב	יָשָׁר	מַלְכָּה
Ab. pl.	סוּסִים	סוּסוֹת	בָּנִים	כּוֹכָבִים	יְשָׁרִים	מְלָכוֹת
Cst. sing.	סוּס	סוּסַת	בֶּן	כּוֹכַב	יְשַׁר	מַלְכַּת
Cst. pl.	סוּסֵי	סוּסוֹת	בְּנֵי	כּוֹכְבֵי	יִשְׁרֵי	מַלְכוֹת
Ab. dual.	סוּסַיִם	סוּסָתַיִם				
Cst. dual.	סוּסֵי	סוּסָתַי				

Since the construct is as short as possible, it is axiomatic that it never takes the article. This latter is put with the absolute noun if it is definite, and in this way suffices for both. For example, סוּס הַמֶּלֶךְ means "the horse of the king" (literally, "horse-of

the-king"), and אִישׁ הַמִּלְחָמָה "the man of war"
(literally, "man-of the war"). Because of the close
relationship between construct and absolute, any
adjectives qualifying the construct will naturally
follow the absolute, and will agree in gender and
number. Thus, "the good mares of the king" would
be rendered סוּסוֹת הַמֶּלֶךְ הַטּוֹבוֹת, *i.e.*, mares-of the
king, the good ones (*f*).

When two absolutes occur, the construct is
repeated with each, as with "the sons of the king and
queen", בְּנֵי הַמֶּלֶךְ וּבְנֵי הַמַּלְכָּה. Adjectives and participles may be placed in the construct before a noun,
thus showing that the construct is not a true genitive,
e.g., "the poor people" is אֶבְיוֹנֵי הָעָם, *i.e.*, the poor
of the people.

The deficiency which exists in the development of
the Hebrew adjective is frequently overcome by the
use of a noun in the construct state. Thus the phrase
"a holy mountain" would be rendered "a mountain
of holiness", *i.e.*, הַר־קֹדֶשׁ, and "a godly man" as "a
man of God", אִישׁ־אֱלֹהִים.

The preposition לְ resolves the apparent confusion
which might arise in rendering the expressions "a
horse of the king" and "the horse of a king", for if
the article were attached to the second noun, both
words would become definite. Furthermore, according to our rule above, the construct cannot take the

article.   Thus these phrases would be translated סוּס
לַמֶּ֫לֶךְ, "a horse belonging to the king", and הַסּוּס לְמֶ֫לֶךְ,
"the horse belonging to a king".

VOCABULARY

שָׁלוֹם	peace.	דָּוִד	David.	עֶ֫בֶד	servant.
פַּרְעֹה	Pharaoh.	שָׁנָה	year.	יַעֲקֹב	Jacob.
עַל־	upon, over.	שָׁאוּל	Saul.	יָשָׁר	upright.
חַיִּים	life (*pl.*).	תָּמִים	perfect.	בָּשָׂר	flesh.
אַבְרָהָם	Abraham.	קָדוֹשׁ	holy.	קָבַץ	to gather.

Exercise 12

Translate :

‎1. סוּסוֹת הַמֶּ֫לֶךְ הַטּוֹבוֹת.   2. לָקַח הַנָּבִיא סוּס אֲשֶׁר לַמֶּ֫לֶךְ.
‎3. אֵ֫לֶּה יְמֵי שְׁנֵי חַיֵּי הַמֶּ֫לֶךְ הָרָע.   4. נָתַן אֱלֹהִים אֶת־הַשֶּׁ֫מֶשׁ
בִּרְקִיעַ הַשָּׁמַ֫יִם.   5. אָמַר עֶ֫בֶד אַבְרָהָם אָנֹכִי.   6. וְעַל־פְּנֵי כָּל־
הַנְּבִיאִים יִשְׁכֹּן.   7. שָׁמַ֫רְתָּ אֶת־לֵבַב הַמֶּ֫לֶךְ הַגָּדוֹל מֵרָע
‎8. לֹא שָׁמַע הָעָם אֶת־דִּבְרֵי נְבִיאֵי הָאֱלֹהִים.   9. חֶ֫רֶב הַזָּהָב בְּיַד
הַגִּבּוֹר.   10. לֹא זְכַרְתֶּם אֶת הַדְּבָרִים אֲשֶׁר אָמְרוּ בְּנֵי נְבִיאֵי
הָאֱלֹהִים.

1. The God of heaven and earth.   2. The voice of God
is in the city of David.   3. The eyes of the man are upon
the horses of Pharaoh.   4. The words of the people are very
bad in the ears of the prophet.   5. The horse which belongs
to the good king is in the desert.   6. The mighty man of
Saul slew the prophets of Jehovah in the place where David
dwelt.   7. I am no prophet, neither am I a prophet's son.
8. And he said, I am the God of Abraham, the God of
Isaac and the God of Jacob.   9. The law of Jehovah is
good in the eyes of the people.   10. Hast thou(*f*) eaten
from the tree which is in the garden of Jehovah ?

CHAPTER XIV

PRONOMINAL SUFFIXES

THE same closeness of relation observed in the construct state marks the connection between nouns and possessive pronouns. Hebrew does not say "my word", but "word-of me", so that in effect we have the noun in the construct and the pronoun in the absolute. To this end, fragments of the personal pronoun are attached in suffixal form to the noun concerned. There are both singular and plural suffixes, which may be added to singular or plural words. Suffixes may be classed as "light" when they contain one consonant, and "heavy" when two consonants are involved. Suffixal forms are derived as follows :

Masculine Nouns

Singular:		סוּס (horse)	פָּקִיד (overseer)	דָּבָר (word)
Suffix	1 c. my	סוּסִי	פְּקִידִי	דְּבָרִי
sing.	2 m. thy	סוּסְךָ	פְּקִידְךָ	דְּבָרְךָ
	2 f. thy	סוּסֵךְ	פְּקִידֵךְ	דְּבָרֵךְ
	3 m. his	סוּסוֹ	פְּקִידוֹ	דְּבָרוֹ
	3 f. her	סוּסָהּ	פְּקִידָהּ	דְּבָרָהּ
Suffix	1 c. our	סוּסֵנוּ	פְּקִידֵנוּ	דְּבָרֵנוּ
plur.	2 m. your	סוּסְכֶם	פְּקִידְכֶם	דְּבַרְכֶם

2 f. your	סוּסְכֶן	פְּקִידְכֶן	דְּבַרְכֶן
3 m. their	סוּסָם	פְּקִידָם	דְּבָרָם
3 f. their	סוּסָן	פְּקִידָן	דְּבָרָן

Plural. סוּסִים (horses) פְּקִידִים (overseers) דְּבָרִים (words)

Suffix	1. c. my	סוּסַי	פְּקִידַי	דְּבָרַי
sing.	2 m. thy	סוּסֶיךָ	פְּקִידֶיךָ	דְּבָרֶיךָ
	2 f. thy	סוּסַיִךְ	פְּקִידַיִךְ	דְּבָרַיִךְ
	3 m. his	סוּסָיו	פְּקִידָיו	דְּבָרָיו
	3 f. her	סוּסֶיהָ	פְּקִידֶיהָ	דְּבָרֶיהָ
Suffix	1 c. our	סוּסֵינוּ	פְּקִידֵינוּ	דְּבָרֵינוּ
plur.	2 m. your	סוּסֵיכֶם	פְּקִידֵיכֶם	דִּבְרֵיכֶם
	2 f. your	סוּסֵיכֶן	פְּקִידֵיכֶן	דִּבְרֵיכֶן
	3 m. their	סוּסֵיהֶם	פְּקִידֵיהֶם	דִּבְרֵיהֶם
	3 f. their	סוּסֵיהֶן	פְּקִידֵיהֶן	דִּבְרֵיהֶן

Feminine Nouns

Singular. סוּסָה (mare) שָׁנָה (year) צְדָקָה (righteous-ness)

Suffix	1.c. my	סוּסָתִי	שְׁנָתִי	צִדְקָתִי
sing.	2 m. thy	סוּסָתְךָ	שְׁנָתְךָ	צִדְקָתְךָ
	2 f. thy	סוּסָתֵךְ	שְׁנָתֵךְ	צִדְקָתֵךְ
	3 m. his	סוּסָתוֹ	שְׁנָתוֹ	צִדְקָתוֹ
	3 f. her	סוּסָתָה	שְׁנָתָה	צִדְקָתָה
Suffix	1 c. our	סוּסָתֵנוּ	שְׁנָתֵנוּ	צִדְקָתֵנוּ
plur.	2 m. your	סוּסַתְכֶם	שְׁנַתְכֶם	צִדְקַתְכֶם
	2 f. your	סוּסַתְכֶן	שְׁנַתְכֶן	צִדְקַתְכֶן
	3 m. their	סוּסָתָם	שְׁנָתָם	צִדְקָתָם
	3 f their	סוּסָתָן	שְׁנָתָן	צִדְקָתָן

Plural.	סוּסוֹת (mares)	שָׁנוֹת (years)	צִדְקוֹת (righteous-nesses)
Suffix sing. 1 c. my	סוּסוֹתַי	שָׁנוֹתַי	צִדְקוֹתַי
2 m. thy	סוּסוֹתֶיךָ	שְׁנוֹתֶיךָ	צִדְקוֹתֶיךָ
2 f. thy	סוּסוֹתַיִךְ	שְׁנוֹתַיִךְ	צִדְקוֹתַיִךְ
3 m. his	סוּסוֹתָיו	שְׁנוֹתָיו	צִדְקוֹתָיו
3 f. her	סוּסוֹתֶיהָ	שְׁנוֹתֶיהָ	צִדְקוֹתֶיהָ
Suffix plur. 1 c. our	סוּסוֹתֵינוּ	שְׁנוֹתֵינוּ	צִדְקוֹתֵינוּ
2 m. your	סוּסוֹתֵיכֶם	שְׁנוֹתֵיכֶם	צִדְקוֹתֵיכֶם
2 f. your	סוּסוֹתֵיכֶן	שְׁנוֹתֵיכֶן	צִדְקוֹתֵיכֶן
3 m. their	סוּסוֹתֵיהֶם	שְׁנוֹתֵיהֶם	צִדְקוֹתֵיהֶם
3 f. their	סוּסוֹתֵיהֶן	שְׁנוֹתֵיהֶן	צִדְקוֹתֵיהֶן

It will be noticed that the šᵉwa in the second masculine singular and second masculine and feminine plural of the singular noun is vocal, and thus bᵉghadhkᵉphath letters will not have dagheš lene. The letter yodh persists in every suffixal form of the plural words. Suffixes for the dual are exactly the same as those of the plural, *i.e.*, שְׂפָתַי, my lips, שְׂפָתֶיךָ, thy (*m.*) lips, etc.

Prepositions may take suffixes in exactly the same way, though feminine forms are sometimes wanting. The following table indicates the inflections of some of the more commonly used prepositions:

Singular	מִן	לְ	עַל	בֵּין	אֶת־	אַחֲרֵי	אֶת (with)
1 c.	מִמֶּנִּי	לִי	עָלַי	בֵּינִי	אֹתִי	אַחֲרַי	אִתִּי
2 m.	מִמְּךָ	לְךָ	עָלֶיךָ	בֵּינְךָ	אֹתְךָ	אַחֲרֶיךָ	אִתְּךָ
2 f.	מִמֵּךְ	לָךְ	עָלַיִךְ	בֵּינֵךְ	אֹתָךְ	אַחֲרַיִךְ	אִתָּךְ

	מִמֶּנּוּ	לוֹ	עָלָיו	בֵּינוֹ	אֹתוֹ	אַחֲרָיו	אֹתוֹ
3 m.	מִמֶּנּוּ	לוֹ	עָלָיו	בֵּינוֹ	אֹתוֹ	אַחֲרָיו	אֹתוֹ
3 f.	מִמֶּנָּה	לָהּ	עָלֶיהָ		אֹתָהּ	אַחֲרֶיהָ	אֹתָהּ
Plural							
1 c.	מִמֶּנּוּ	לָנוּ	עָלֵינוּ	בֵּינֵינוּ	אֹתָנוּ	אַחֲרֵינוּ	אֹתָנוּ
2 m.	מִכֶּם	לָכֶם	עֲלֵיכֶם	בֵּינֵיכֶם	אֶתְכֶם	אַחֲרֵיכֶם	אֶתְכֶם
2 f.		לָכֶן			אֶתְכֶן	אַחֲרֵיכֶן	אֶתְכֶן
3 m.	מֵהֶם	לָהֶם	עֲלֵיהֶם	בֵּינֵיהֶם	אֹתָם	אַחֲרֵיהֶם	אֹתָם
3 f.		לָהֶן			אֹתָן	אַחֲרֵיהֶן	אֹתָן

VOCABULARY

אֵת	with	תַּחַת	under	חָדָשׁ	new
אַחֲרֵי	after	רָדַף	to pursue	יֶלֶד	boy
לִפְנֵי	before	מָכַר	to sell	יָשַׁב	to sit
דָּג	fish	שׁוֹר	ox	בֵּין	between
אֶל־	towards	כֹּהֵן	priest	לֶחֶם	bread

Exercise 13

Translate :

1. מִכֶּם. 2. מִמֶּנּוּ. 3. אַחֲרֶיךָ. 4. אַתָּה. 5. לִפְנֵי הָאִישׁ. 6. סוּסֵיהֶן
7. סוּסוֹתֵיהֶם. 8. צִדְקוֹתֵיכֶן. 9. שָׁמַעְתִּי אֶת־דִּבְרֵיהֶם. 10. יְדֵיכֶם
11. לָהֶם. 12. דִּבְרֵיהֶם הֵם רָעִים בְּעֵינֵי יהוה. 13. שָׁלַח הַנָּבִיא
אֶת־בָּנָיו וְאֶת־בְּנוֹתָיו אֶל־הַמִּדְבָּר. 14. שָׁמְעוּ אֶת־קוֹלְךָ
בְּהֵיכַל הָאֱלֹהִים. 15. בֵּינִי וּבֵינֶךָ. 16. וְלֹא רָדַפְתִּי אַחֲרֵי בְּנֵי
יַעֲקֹב. 17. כִּי שָׁמַרְתִּי אֶת־דַּרְכֵי יהוה אֱלֹהֵי יִשְׂרָאֵל. 18. בְּסֵפֶר
מַלְכֵי יִשְׂרָאֵל וִיהוּדָה. 19. לֹא שָׁמְרוּ אֶת־מִצְוֹת יהוה אֲשֶׁר
נָתַן לָהֶם בָּהָר. 20. וְכָל־מִשְׁפָּטָיו לְפָנֶיךָ.

1. Before me. 2. After them(*f.*). 3. Upon him. 4. From thee(*f.*). 5. Towards you (*m. pl.*). 6. Before you (*m. pl.*). 7. Before thee(*m.*). 8. My face. 9. Our hands. 10. Thy(*f*) lips. 11. Their(*f*) righteousnesses. 12. Our words. 13. Their(*m*) horse. 14. Your(*f*) horses. 15. Your(*f*) mares. 16. Between us. 17. Under him. 18. Behold me. 19. Their(*m*) lips. 20. Thy strong hand is with the people.

CHAPTER XV

THE VERB: OTHER FORMS

In an earlier chapter we examined briefly two of the most important forms of the regular verb, where we recognised that Hebrew has no "tenses" in the normal sense of that word. Instead there are two "states" : the perfect, which expresses any kind of completed action, and the imperfect, which denotes any incomplete action, past, present or future. Thus, the perfect would be used to translate such phrases as "he ate", "he would have eaten", "he had eaten", whilst the imperfect state is reflected in such expressions as "he will eat", "he eats", "he was eating," "he might eat", and so on. To express a development of the basic verbal idea there are in all seven "themes", including active and passive, intensive and causative themes, and a reflexive.

Verbs are spoken of as "strong" where the three radicals do not change, or where one of them is a guttural, and "weak" where either one radical is assimilated or where a verb ends in a weak consonant, *e.g.*, ה. The "stative" verbs are so called because they generally describe the state, physical or mental, of the subject, *e.g.*, to be heavy, to be old. Usually they are intransitive, but not wholly so, and the term "stative" must not be taken as synonymous with "intransitive". We can now study some special forms of the verb in subsequent sections.

The Imperative

When the preformatives are dropped, the imperative Qal is identical with the imperfect. It is important to notice that the šᵉwa in the first syllable is sounded, making the syllable open in each case. The imperative is never used with the negative to express a prohibition, being employed exclusively for positive commands, *e.g.*, מִשְׁלוּ, rule ye.

The Jussive

This is in speech a shortened form of the imperfect to express the quick reaction of the mind to a situation, generally in terms of a wish or a command. It coincides with the imperfect in form in all parts of the regular verb except the hiph'il (or causative) but is used only in the second and third persons. Its negative is אַל, not לֹא. It is used mainly :

(a) To express a positive command in the third person, *e.g.*, יְהִי אוֹר, let there be light.

(b) As a request or entreaty, *e.g.*, אַל תִּקְטֹל, do not thou (*m.*) kill.

(c) As a prohibition, *e.g.*, אַל־תִּקְטְלוּ, do not kill. When Divine prohibitions are recorded, the negative לֹא is used in the sense of "thou shalt not", often with the simple imperfect, *e.g.*, לֹא תִרְצָח (Deut. v. 17), "thou shalt not kill", as a permanent prohibition.

The Cohortative

This form is generally confined to the first person singular and plural, and in speech tends to lessen the abruptness of a command, to exhort, or to express the resolution of the speaker. It is marked by the ending הָ‑ added to the imperfect, *e.g.*, נִשְׁמְרָה let us keep, we would keep. An emphatic imperative particle, נָא, is frequently added to the Cohortative, Jussive and Imperative, as well as to particles such as הִנֵּה (behold!), to introduce an additional supplicatory note, or to strengthen the exhortation, *e.g.*, בֹּא־נָא, go, I pray.

Waw Consecutive

The comparative scarcity of subordinate clauses in Hebrew, combined with the limited modifications of the verb, made it necessary to employ a special device for denoting sequence of events in connected clauses or sentences. The effect is to introduce a subordinating quality into the initial verb of the sentence or phrase, so that what happens as a result is in direct sequence to the general tenor of the preceding verb.

In this construction, a consecutive narrative of past events which commences with a perfect tense is continued by a succession of imperfects coupled with waw, which is pointed like the article under such conditions. Conversely, when such a sentence begins with a simple imperfect, successive events are expressed by means of waw with the perfect, when the pointing for waw is exactly the same as for the conjunction וְ.

Thus, in the sentence "he went out and pursued and captured", the initial verb is in the perfect, but since the succession of events depends so intimately upon it, they are expressed by the waw consecutive form, יָצָא וַיִּרְדֹּף וַיִּלְכֹּד. Where, however, the sequence is disrupted, the tense reverts to the perfect, as may be seen from a continuation of the above sentence, "he went out and pursued and captured, and did not rest in the city", which would now become יָצָא וַיִּרְדֹּף וַיִּלְכֹּד וְלֹא שָׁבַת בָּעִיר. Here the negative intervenes between waw and the verb "rest", which according to our rule necessitates a reversion to the perfect form.

Similarly, in a sentence commencing with an imperfect, subsequent verbs are perfect if immediately preceded by waw, e.g., "he will remember the prophets, and will go out and hear them in the temple", which is rendered יִזְכֹּר אֶת־הַנְּבִיאִים וְיָצָא

וְשָׁמַע אַתָּם בַּהֵיכָל. Again, if a word intervenes between waw and the verb, the latter reverts to the tense of the first verb in the series.

It is important to grasp these principles clearly, as the waw consecutive is found very widely in the Hebrew of the Old Testament. We may summarise the matter as follows :

(a) After a simple perfect, connected successive verbs have waw with the imperfect.

(b) After a simple imperfect, verbs consequent upon it have waw with the perfect.

In Hebrew narrative, the verb הָיָה, to be or become, is usually followed by waw consecutive when other words occur between the two verbs. The imperfect of הָיָה (יְהְיֶה) has a shortened form, יְהִי, used with waw consecutive, i.e., וַיְהִי, the daghes forte usually being omitted with יְ. In such a usage the verb "to be" is generally rendered "and it came to pass", e.g., . . . וַיְהִי אַחֲרֵי הַדְּבָרִים הָאֵלֶּה וָיָקָם, "and it came to pass after these words that he arose . . ."

In the imperfect with waw consecutive, the accentuation is generally mil'el when the penultimate is open, e.g., וַיֵּשֶׁב, and he dwelt. Conversely, the perfect with waw consecutive has a milra' accentuation wherever possible, e.g., וְשָׁמַרְתָּ, and thou wilt keep. Sometimes waw consecutive marks the consequent clause in a conditional sentence, *e.g.*, . . . אִם־עָבַרְתָּ אִתִּי וְהָיִיתָ עָלַי, "if thou passest on with me, then thou shalt be to me . . . " (2 Sam. xv. 33).

A "weak" waw, or one which does not influence the form of the verb, is normally only found in the third person of the Jussive (וְיִקְטֹל, and let him kill) and with the Cohortative (וְאֶקְטְלָה, and let me kill).

The Infinitive

There are two infinitives in Hebrew, known as the absolute and construct, of which the latter is the more common. The infinitive absolute stands entirely alone, having neither prefix nor suffix, and serves principally to emphasise the verb. Thus the sentence "he hath indeed kept my commandments" would be rendered in Hebrew "in-the-act-of-keeping he has kept my commandments", *i.e.*, שָׁמוֹר שָׁמַר אֶת מִצְוֹתַי. It has thus an adverbial force, like "truly", "certainly", "surely", and as such generally stands in order before the verb. On the occasions when it occurs after the finite verb it expresses continuity, *e.g.*, שִׁמְעוּ שָׁמוֹעַ, "hear ye continually". Infrequently it expresses the imperative sense, as in the injunction "keep the sabbath day", שָׁמוֹר אֶת־יוֹם הַשַּׁבָּת.

Unlike the absolute form, the construct may have a preposition prefixed, as well as pronominal suffixes. Most frequently the infinitive construct takes the preposition לְ as a prefix, *e.g.*, לִשְׁפֹּט, to judge, expressing the English infinitive "to". The dagheš lene is inserted in the second radical only with לְ, and with other prepositions the first syllable remains open, *e.g.*, בִּשְׁפֹּט. The construct is negatived by removing לְ and prefixing it to בִּלְתִּי ("so as not to"), which then precedes the infinitive, *i.e.*, לְבִלְתִּי שְׁמֹעַ, (so as) not to listen. Often the infinitive is connected by maqqeph to its object, *e.g.*, לִכְרֹת־עֵצִים, to cut down trees. In form it is generally the same as the second singular of the imperative. The suffixes of the infinitive construct may be illustrated by the use of the verb כָּתַב to write:

	Singular	Plural
1 c.	כָּתְבִי כָּתְבֵנִי	כָּתְבֵנוּ
2 m.	כָּתְבְּךָ כָּתְבְךָ	כָּתְבְּכֶם כָּתְבְכֶם
2 f.	כָּתְבֵךְ	כָּתְבְּכֶן כָּתְבְכֶן
3 m.	כָּתְבוֹ	כָּתְבָם
3 f.	כָּתְבָהּ	כָּתְבָן

Hebrew idiom would say "in-the-writing-of-me" for "when I wrote", hence the value of the suffixal form for showing the gerund-like nature of the infinitive construct.

The Participle

In the regular verb there are two forms of the participle, the active (קֹטֵל, killing) and the passive (קָטוּל, killed). For their inflections in gender and number they are regarded as nouns, thus :

	Singular		Plural	
	Absol.	Cstr.	Absol.	Cstr.
Active m.	קֹטֵל	קֹטֵל	קֹטְלִים	קֹטְלֵי
f.	קֹטְלָה, קֹטֶלֶת	קֹטֶלֶת	קֹטְלוֹת	קֹטְלוֹת
Passive m.	קָטוּל	קְטוּל	קְטוּלִים	קְטוּלֵי
f.	קְטוּלָה	קְטוּלַת	קְטוּלוֹת	קְטוּלוֹת

The holem in these forms is invariably long.

They are frequently used as ordinary substantives, and as such belong to distinct groups of nouns whose changes will be noted in a later chapter. The participles imply continuous activity, and this is especially true of the active form. In meaning they are like gerundives or verbal adjectives, and may agree in gender and number with a noun or pronoun, e.g., אֲנַחְנוּ מֹשְׁלִים, we are ruling. When the third radical of a verb is a guttural, a furtive pathah appears with the passive participle, e.g., יָדוּעַ, known. On occasions the passive participle may have a future connotation, e.g., שָׁדוּד, that which ought to be destroyed. The negative אֵין is generally used with participles instead of לֹא.

VOCABULARY

כִּי אִם	except.	נָהָר	river.	פָּקַד	to visit.
יָצָא	to go out.	כָּבוֹד	glory.	נָפַל	to fall.
קָצַף	to be angry.	גָּנַב	to steal.	מֵת	dead.
קוּם	to arise, stand.	נָשָׂא	to lift up.	אֶבְיוֹן	poor.
עָבַר	to pass over, cross.	פֶּן	lest.	זָכָר	male.

Exercise 14

Translate:

‎1. אַל תִּקְצֹף‎ ‎2. לֹא תִּגְנֹב‎ ‎3. אִמְרָה־נָּא‎ ‎4. וַיֹּאמֶר אֱלֹהִים‎
‎נֹפֵל לְפָנַי וְלֹא אֶקְצֹף בְּךָ עַד־עוֹלָם‎ ‎5. רָדְפוּ אַחֲרָיו‎ ‎6. אַל‎
‎יִכָּתֵב בְּסֵפֶר תּוֹרַת יהוה אֱלֹהֵי יִשְׂרָאֵל‎ ‎7. הָלַכְתִּי וָאֹמַר‎
‎אֶת־הַיֶּלֶד‎ ‎8. שָׁכַח הָאִישׁ אֶת־דִּבְרֵי הַנָּבִיא וְלֹא שָׁמַר אֶת־‎
‎תּוֹרַת יהוה‎ ‎9. וַיִּתֵּן אֹתוֹ עַל־כָּל־אֶרֶץ מִצְרָיִם‎ ‎10. שָׁמוֹר‎
‎יִשְׁמֹר אֶת־תּוֹרַת אֱלֹהִים‎ ‎11. וְכֹר הַנָּבִיא אֶת־הַדְּבָרִים‎
‎הָאֵלֶּה וַיֹּאמֶר רְדֹף אַחֲרֵיהֶם צְפוֹנָה‎ ‎12. אַתֶּם זְכָרִים אֶת־‎
‎דִּבְרֵי הָאֱלֹהִים אֲשֶׁר אָמַרְתִּי בַּיּוֹם הַזֶּה‎ ‎13. הִנְנִי שֹׁלֵחַ אֶת־‎
‎הַנָּבִיא הָעִירָה.‎

1. Thou shalt keep my commandments. 2. May he keep thee from all evil in the land. 3. Let me go, I pray, to the house of the prophet. 4. And God made the firmament between the waters which were under the firmament, and between the waters which were above the firmament. 5. Let me keep thy commandments. 6. He kept on walking towards the house of Joseph. 7. I will

keep thy commandments continually.   8. They left off
counting the stars of heaven.   9. They went down to
Egypt to buy food in that place.   10. And behold, he
sent the boy to watch the city of the mighty men.   11.
Jehovah is thy keeper in the day of evil.   12. The prophets
are keeping the law of Jehovah, the God of Israel.   13. The
king rules over the people in the land.

CHAPTER XVI

PARADIGM OF THE REGULAR VERB

IN the last chapter we noted that there are a number
of "themes" which serve to convey a developed idea
of the simple verb, and these must now be given
somewhat closer scrutiny. Their names are a
reminder of the time when פָּעַל was used to illustrate
the paradigm of the regular verb, since the "themes"
are named according to the corresponding inflection
of פָּעַל ın the third singular masculine of the perfect.
Thus the simple passive of פָּעַל would be נִפְעַל, and
so the passive voice in the regular verb is called the
Niphʻal. קָטַל has replaced פָּעַל as the standard form
for the verb paradigm because פָּעַל, having the
second radical a guttural, is thus unable to take
dagheš forte in three important forms of the strong
or regular verb. The various forms, whose full
inflections will be found in the paradigm section at
the end of the book, are as follows :

Simple active or Qal.	קָטַל
Simple passive or Niphʻal.	נִקְטַל
Intensive active or Piʻel.	קִטֵּל
Intensive passive or Puʻal.	קֻטַּל
Causative active or Hiphʻil.	הִקְטִיל
Causative passive or Hophʻal.	הָקְטַל
Reflexive or Hithpaʻel.	הִתְקַטֵּל

These forms are derived by internal changes of the root and other modifications. The second radical of the Pi'el, Pu'al and Hithpa'el has dagheš forte to intensify the form. The Pu'al and Hoph'al lack an imperative and infinitive construct, and with the exception of the Niph'al, all participles have a prefixed מ.

Niph'al.

In the perfect, the letter נ is prefixed to the stem and pointed with hireq, whilst the imperfect has a prefixed יִ with the nun becoming assimilated to the first radical, which then takes a compensating dagheš forte, i.e., יִקָּטֵל. The imperative is marked by a prefix הִן, which by assimilation becomes הִקָּטֵל. Before a vowel suffix the çere under the second radical becomes vocal šᵉwa, except in pause, i.e., הִקָּטְלִי but in the second feminine plural it changes to pathah, i.e., הִקָּטַלְנָה. This latter becomes qameç in pause. The infinitive construct is like the imperative, but in the absolute the çere is replaced by holem, הִקָּטֹל, with an alternative form נִקְטֹל. The Niph'al participle may have gerundive force, and as such is often used for phrases with a passive meaning, e.g., the broken of heart, would be וְשִׁבְרֵי־לֵב, i.e., the broken ones of heart, with "heart" appearing normally in such an expression in the shorter form in preference to לֵבָב. The Niph'al is inflected like the Qal.

The primary force of the Niph‘al is reflexive, *e.g.*, נִסְתַּר he hid himself, though it is found in a reciprocal or "middle" sense, *e.g.*, נִלְחֲמוּ, they fought (one another), and predominantly as the simple passive of the Qal.　מִן, בְּ and לְ are used as the agent when the Niph‘al, has a passive force.　Some verbs are used only in the Niph‘al *e.g.*, נִלְחַם, he fought, without any reflexive or passive meaning.

Pi‘el

A dagheš forte in the middle radical is characteristic of this form.　In the first syllable the vowel is generally hireq, whilst the second syllable may have pathah or çere.　In three verbs, כִּבֵּס, he washed, כִּפֶּר, he atoned, and דִּבֶּר, he spoke, sᵉghol replaces çere. The imperfect יְקַטֵּל is inflected regularly, whilst of the infinitives, the absolute קַטֹּל is less frequently used than the form קַטֵּל, which is the same as that of the construct.　The participle has a prefixed מ, pointed with šᵉwa.　The Pi‘el is inflected like the Qal.

The Pi‘el is an intensive form of the Qal, *e.g.*, רָדַף, to follow, רִדַּף, to pursue.　Where intensity becomes iteration, a causative force may be evident, *e.g.*, גָּדַל, to be great, גִּדַּל, to cause to be great, make great ; קָדַשׁ, to be holy, קִדַּשׁ, to hallow.

Pu‘al

This form is marked by dull vocalic sounds, but like the Pi‘el has regular inflections.　In the perfect, qibbuç is found under the first radical, whilst the pathah of the second radical becomes vocal šᵉwa before vowel afformatives. In this latter respect the imperfect is similar. There is no imperative form of the Puʻal, since it is properly the passive of the Piʻel in meaning.

VOCABULARY

לחם	to fight (Niph.).	זֶבַח	sacrifice.	יְאֹר	river.
אֱמֹרִי	Amorites.	חָבַשׁ	to bind, gird.	בְּכוֹר	firstborn.
נחם	to repent (Niph.).	אָרַר	to curse.	כֹּה	thus.
קָטֹן	small, little.	בקשׁ	to seek (Pi.).	זָקֵן	old, elder.
כסה	to conceal (Pi.).	סתר	to hide (Pi.).	זָבַח	to sacrifice.
צֶלֶם	image, likeness.	יָכֹל	to be able.	אַהֲרֹן	Aaron.
זְרוֹעַ	arm.	שָׁתָה	to drink.	כָּבֵד	to be heavy ; (Pi.) to harden

Exercise 15

Translate :

1. וַיֹּאמֶר יהוה אֵלַי אֱמֹר לָהֶם לֹא תִלָּחֲמוּ 2. וְשַׁבְתֶּם בַּמָּקוֹם הַהוּא יָמִים רַבִּים 3. וַיִּנָּחֶם יהוה כִּי עָשָׂה אֶת־הָאָדָם בָּאָרֶץ 4. וַיְכַסּוּ כָּל־הֶהָרִים הַגְּדוֹלִים אֲשֶׁר־תַּחַת כָּל־הַשָּׁמַיִם 5. וְזִבְחֵי אֱלֹהִים רוּחַ נִשְׁבָּרָה 6. תִּשְׁלַח לְעַבְדְּךָ לֵב שֹׁמֵעַ לִשְׁפֹּט

אֶת־עַמְּךָ הַזֶּה   7.   בֶּן־אָדָם שָׁבַרְתִּי אֶת־זְרוֹעַ פַּרְעֹה מֶלֶךְ

מִצְרַיִם וְהִנֵּה לֹא־חֻבָּשָׁה   8.   אָמַרְתָּ בַּקְשׁוּ פָנָי אֶת־פָּנֶיךָ

אֲבַקֵּשׁ   9.   וְעַתָּה אָרוּר אַתָּה מִן־הָאֲדָמָה אֲשֶׁר בָּרָא הָאֱלֹהִים

10.   וַיְכַבֵּד פַּרְעֹה אֶת־לִבּוֹ וְלֹא שִׁלַּח אֶת־הָעָם.

1. And the Amorites which dwelt in that mountain sent
and pursued you. 2. Do not fight (*pl.*) with small or great,
but only (except) with the king of Israel. 3. And God
said, Shall I conceal (*part.*) from Abraham that which I
have done? 4. The one shedding man's blood, by man
shall his blood be shed, for in the image of God he made
man. 5. And in the books of the house of Israel they shall
not be written. 6. Behold thou hast sent me this day
from upon the face of the ground, and from thy face shall
I be hidden. 7. They were not able to drink of the waters
of the river. 8. And thou shalt say unto Pharaoh, thus
said the Lord, My son, even my firstborn, is Israel. 9.
And they will hear thy voice, and thou shalt come, thou
and the elders of Israel, to the king of Egypt, and ye shall
say unto him, Let us go, we pray, unto the desert that
we may sacrifice to the Lord our God. 10. And Aaron
spoke all the words which Jehovah said unto Moses.

CHAPTER XVII

PARADIGM OF THE REGULAR VERB

(*continued*)

Hiph'il

This is the active causative form, and in the perfect consists of the verb stem prefixed by ה and the vowel hireq (which occasionally becomes sᵉghol), with the insertion of a full hireq between the second and third radicals, *i.e.*, הִקְטִיל.

The Imperfect has the same final syllable, but takes pathah under the initial letter, thus, יַקְטִיל. It should be noticed that in the Hiph'il only there exists a difference between the ordinary imperfect and the jussive (יַקְטֵל). The çere may be shortened to sᵉghol in the jussive if the tone alters in position, *e.g.*, from יַקְטֵל to יַקְטֶל־. The inflection of the Hiph'il is regular.

Its typical meaning is the causative of the Qal, *e.g.*, קָדַשׁ, to be holy, הִקְדִּישׁ, to cause to be holy, to sanctify. It may also have a declaratory meaning, as with הִצְדִּיק, he pronounced righteous. Stative verbs frequently appear in the Hiph'il, *e.g.*, הִשְׁמִין, to become fat. If the Qal of the verb is transitive, the Hiph'il may govern two accusatives in a sentence, *e.g.*, הִנְחִיל אֹתָם אֶת־הָאָרֶץ, he caused them to inherit the land.

Hoph'al

The first syllable of this form is always closed, as with the Hiph'il, though sometimes the qameç hatuph may be replaced by qibbuç, and this is especially the case with the participle, *e.g.*, מֻקְטָל for מָקְטָל.

The Hoph'al is inflected in the normal manner, and since it is passive in meaning it has no regular imperative form.

Hithpa'el

This is formed by prefixing הִת to the Pi'el, with pathah under the first radical, *e.g.*, הִתְקַטֵּל. When a sibilant follows the prefix, the sibilant and the taw of the prefix exchange places thus, הִשְׁתַּמֵּר, for הִתְשַׁמֵּר, he was on his guard. With צ and ז the taw is replaced by the appropriate hard or soft lingual, *e.g.*, הִצְטַדֵּק for הִתְצַדֵּק, and הִזְדַּמֵּן for הִתְזַמֵּן.

In meaning it is primarily the reflexive of the Pi'el, *e.g.*, נָקַם, he avenged, הִתְנַקֵּם, he showed himself revengeful. It may also express reciprocal action, *e.g.*, הִתְרָאָא, they looked at each other, and infrequently may be intransitive and similar in force to the Qal, *e.g.*, הִתְאַבֵּל, to mourn. Another connotation is that of "playing the part of" something, *e.g.*, הִתְחַכַּם, he pretended to be a wise man ; הִתְנַבֵּא, he behaved like a prophet.

At this juncture it may be advisable to notice the structure of some rare intensive and causative formations of the verb. Occasionally full holem is inserted in the intensives between the first and second radical to form the Po'el (קוֹטֵל), the Po'al (קוֹטַל) and the Hithpo'el (הִתְקוֹטֵל). Some intensive formations have the third radical doubled, and these are the Pi'lel (קְטְלֵל), the Pu'lal (קְטְלַל) and the Hithpa'lel (הִתְקַטְלֵל). Where the last two stem letters are repeated, the form is called the Pe'al'al (קְטַלְטַל). The Pilpel repeats the first and third radicals (קְלְקֵל). These forms are comparatively rare in their incidence, and there are one or two others connected with the Hiph'il which are even less frequently found.

VOCABULARY

שחת destroy (Hiph.).	כָּשַׁל to stumble.	רָשָׁע wicked, guilty.
בּוֹא to enter.	אָדוֹן lord, master.	קָבַר to bury.
עֵץ tree, twig.	קֶבֶר grave.	כֵּן so, thus.
פֶּתַח opening, gate.	(יֵשׁ‍־), יֵשׁ there is.	חבא (Hith.) to hide oneself.
קָשַׁשׁ to gather, collect.	שׁלךְ (Hiph.) to cast.	תָּוֶךְ middle.
מות to kill, put to death.	בְּתוֹךְ among, within.	אַיִן no, none.

מֶלֶךְ to be king;   קָדֵשׁ to be holy;   חָזַק to be strong;
(Hiph.) to   (Pi.) to   (Hith.) to
make king.   hallow,   take courage.
                       sanctify.

Exercise 16

Translate:

1. וַיֹּאמֶר יהוה אֶל־שְׁמוּאֵל שְׁמַע בְּקוֹלָם וְהִמְלַכְתָּ לָהֶם מֶלֶךְ
2. רָבָא אֶל־פֶּתַח הָעִיר וְהִנֵּה שָׁם אִשָּׁה מְקֹשֶׁשֶׁת עֵצִים 3. וְאַתֶּם
הִכְשַׁלְתֶּם רַבִּים בְּתוֹרַת יהוה 4. וְהִנֵּה אֲדֹנֵיהֶם נֹפֵל אַרְצָה מֵת
5. וְאַתָּה הָשְׁלַכְתָּ מִן־הַשָּׁמַיִם בְּכָל־אֲשֶׁר עָשָׂה אֶת הָרָע 6. וַיֹּאמֶר
יַעֲקֹב לְבָנָיו לָמָּה תִּתְרָאוּ הִנֵּה שָׁמַעְתִּי כִּי יֶשׁ־לֶחֶם בְּמִצְרַיִם
7. וַיֹּאמְרוּ הִתְהַלַּכְנוּ בָאָרֶץ וְהִנֵּה כָל־הָאָרֶץ יֹשֶׁבֶת 8. הִיא הָעִיר
הַפְּקֻדָה בְּיַד יהוה אֱלֹהֵי יִשְׂרָאֵל 9. וְכִשְׁמֹעַ הַנָּבִיא אֶת הַדְּבָרִים
הָאֵלֶּה הִתְחַזַּק 10. רָאִיתִי אֶת־הָרְשָׁעִים קְבֻרִים וַיִּשְׁתַּכְּחוּ בָּעִיר
אֲשֶׁר־כֵּן־עָשׂוּ שָׁם.

1. There entered a man of the people to destroy the king. 2. Thou art come to me to bring to remembrance my sin and to slay my son. 3. These are the luminaries in the firmament of heaven to divide between the day and the night. 4. And he shall be laid (Hoph.) in his grave in the place which the king has given him. 5. And Joshua said to the people, Sanctify yourselves, for Jehovah is in this place. 6. His head was cast upon the ground by the hand of the mighty man. 7. And they heard the voice of Jehovah walking about in the garden. 8. And the man and his wife hid themselves from before the Lord God amongst the trees of the garden. 9. And Pharaoh said, Behold, the people of the land are many, and you make them rest themselves in this place. 10. And they prophesied unto the evening, and there was no voice.

CHAPTER XVIII

DECLENSIONS OF NOUNS

It is generally found convenient to classify nouns in declensions, according to the changes which take place in the vowels when the tone is altered. The first declension, which we have already noticed, deals principally with nouns having qameç in the tone, the pretone, or both. Such nouns are similar to the perfect of the verb.

The second declension, which has affinity to the imperfect, consists of words formed from stems which originally terminated in two consonants but to which an auxiliary vowel, usually sᵉghol, has been added. For this reason they are called "sᵉgholates", and fall into three principal classes, governed by the original vowel. The "a" class is like יֶלֶד, formed from יַלְד; the "e" class is illustrated by סֵפֶר, from an original סִפְר; whilst the "o" class is represented by חֹדֶשׁ, formed from חָדְשׁ.

In inflection the singular construct is the same as the absolute. For the singular of the noun, the suffixes are added to the stem, and the dual is formed in exactly the same way. But the plural absolute has qameç under the second radical, and the first vowel then becomes šᵉwa to accord with the tone.

The following table will illustrate these changes :

	" a " class	" e " class	" o " class
Singular abs. cstr.	יֶ֫לֶד	סֵ֫פֶר	חֹ֫דֶשׁ
light suff.	יַלְדִּי	סִפְרִי	חָדְשִׁי
heavy suff.	יַלְדְּכֶם	סִפְרְכֶם	חָדְשְׁכֶם
Plural abs.	יְלָדִים	סְפָרִים	חֳדָשִׁים
cstr.	יַלְדֵי	סִפְרֵי	חָדְשֵׁי
light suff.	יְלָדַי	סְפָרַי	חֳדָשַׁי
heavy suff.	יַלְדֵיכֶם	סִפְרֵיכֶם	חָדְשֵׁיכֶם
Dual absol.	רַגְלַיִם	בִּרְכַּיִם	אָזְנַיִם
cstr.	רַגְלֵי	בִּרְכֵּי	אָזְנֵי
light suff.	רַגְלַי	בִּרְכַּי	אָזְנַי
heavy suff.	רַגְלֵיכֶם	בִּרְכֵּיכֶם	אָזְנֵיכֶם

These nouns are inflected regularly, but care should be taken to ensure the proper recognition of the šᵉwa, whether silent or vocal. When the terminal letter is a guttural, the preference for pathah is noticed throughout, e.g., זֶרַע, seed, זַרְעִי, my seed, זַרְעֲךָ, thy seed, etc. The absence of an auxiliary sᵉghol in this type of noun indicates something of the inadequacy of the term "sᵉgholates" as a class designation.

Feminine sᵉgholates are formed by adding הָ‎ to the original or primitive stem, e.g., מַלְכָּה‎, queen, and in the singular are formed regularly. The plural has וֹת‎ added to the masculine singular, e.g., מְלָכוֹת‎, and the construct is inflected normally, i.e., מַלְכוֹת‎. Some feminines have a primitive ת‎ as the final letter attached to the stem, e.g., מִשְׁמֶרֶת‎, which takes suffixes in the normal manner, e.g., מִשְׁמַרְתִּי‎, etc. A group of feminine nouns, mostly prefixed by מ‎, have an ending הָ‎, e.g., מַמְלָכָה‎, kingdom. The construct singular becomes sᵉgholate, i.e., מַמְלֶכֶת‎, with suffix, מַמְלַכְתִּי‎, whilst the plural is מַמְלָכוֹת‎.

A third declension may be made up of words similar in form to the active participles. Such nouns generally have an unchangeable vowel in the penultimate, and a tone long çere in the ultimate syllable. They are declined like participles, whose form has already been noted in Chapter XV. Some nouns are not participial in form, and generally relinquish the çere in declensions, e.g., מִזְבֵּחַ‎, altar, cstr. sing. מִזְבַּח‎, suffix מִזְבְּחִי‎, plur. מִזְבְּחוֹת‎, with suffix מִזְבְּחוֹתַי‎, etc.

We may now notice the inflections of some irregular nouns which belong to the various declensions. Where relevant, the particular one is indicated by number.

SINGULAR

	father	son (3)	daughter (2)	brother	name	house (2)
Sing. abs.	אָב	בֵּן	בַּת	אָח	שֵׁם	בַּיִת
constr.	אֲבִי	בֶּן־	בַּת	אֲחִי	שֵׁם, שֶׁם־	בֵּית
suffix	אָבִי	בְּנִי	בִּתִּי	אָחִי	שְׁמִי	בֵּיתִי
	אָבִיךָ	בִּנְךָ	בִּתְּךָ	אָחִיךָ	שִׁמְךָ	בֵּיתְךָ
	אָבִיו	בְּנוֹ	בִּתּוֹ	אָחִיו	שְׁמוֹ	בֵּיתוֹ

PLURAL

	father	son	daughter	brother	name	house
Plur. abs.	אָבוֹת	בָּנִים	בָּנוֹת	אַחִים	שֵׁמוֹת	בָּתִּים
cstr.	אֲבוֹת	בְּנֵי	בְּנוֹת	אֲחֵי	שְׁמוֹת	בָּתֵּי
suffix.	אֲבוֹתַי	בָּנַי	בְּנוֹתַי	אַחַי	שְׁמוֹתַי	בָּתֵּי

SINGULAR

	wife	sister	mouth	man	day (2)	city (2)
Sing. abs.	אִשָּׁה	אָחוֹת	פֶּה	אִישׁ	יוֹם	עִיר
cstr.	אֵשֶׁת	אֲחוֹת	פִּי	אִישׁ	יוֹם	עִיר
suffix	אִשְׁתִּי	אֲחוֹתִי	פִּי	אִישִׁי	יוֹמִי	עִירִי
	אִשְׁתְּךָ		פִּיךָ		יוֹמְךָ	עִירְךָ

PLURAL

	wife	sister	mouth	man	day (2)	city (2)
Plur. abs	נָשִׁים	(אֲחָיוֹת)	פִּיּוֹת	אֲנָשִׁים	יָמִים	עָרִים
cstr.	נְשֵׁי	אַחְיוֹת	פִּיּוֹת	אַנְשֵׁי	יְמֵי	עָרֵי
suffix	נָשַׁי	אַחְיוֹתַי		אֲנָשַׁי	יָמַי	עָרַי

VOCABULARY

צֶדֶק righteous-ness.	גֹּדֶל greatness.	מַלְאָךְ messenger.
קֶשֶׁת bow (f).	חָכְמָה wisdom (f).	חַיִל force, army.
כֶּרֶם vineyard.	עֵצָה counsel (f).	עֵגֶל calf.
רֶגֶל foot (f).	נְקָמָה vengeance (f).	שִׁפְחָה handmaid (f).
שָׂפָה lip (f).	עַתָּה now, shortly.	בֶּרֶךְ knee (f).

Exercise 17

Translate :

‏5. בִּלְבָבוֹ   4. מְקוֹמוֹתֵיכֶם   3. שְׁנֵיהֶם   2. מַלְאָכָיו   1. רַגְלַיִם‏

‏10. שׁוֹרֵיהֶן   9. מֵימֵיהֶם   8. וְנָשֵׁיהֶם   7. עֲצוּתֵיו   6. עֶגְלְךָ‏

‏15. בִּרְכַּיִם   14. כַּרְמִי   13. עָרֵיהֶן   12. פִּיכֶם   11. שִׂפְחוֹתֶיךָ‏

1. Two eyes.   2. Two ears.   3. Their(m) hands.   4. Your(m) blessing.   5. Their(m) words.   6. Your(m) brother. 7. Their(f) houses.   8. Their(m) daughters.   9. My(m) brothers.   10. Their(m) heads.   11. His righteousness. 12. Their(m) calves.   13. My greatness.   14. Your(m) king. 15. Our armies.

CHAPTER XIX

DEGREES OF COMPARISON: NUMERALS

In a relatively primitive and simple language such as Hebrew it would be out of place to expect special forms to indicate degrees of comparison. It is possible, however, to express such ideas, though a certain amount of circumlocution is involved.

The comparative degree of superiority or inferiority is expressed by attaching the preposition מִן after the positive adjective to the word with which the noun is being compared, e.g., גָּדוֹל מִן־דָּוִד, greater than David; טוֹב מֵאַבְרָהָם, better than Abraham, where מִן ("from") has the force of "in comparison with".

The superlative degree may be indicated in a number of ways, as follows:

(a) By prefixing the article to the positive adjective coming after a definite noun, e.g., הַבֵּן הַגָּדוֹל, the eldest son (i.e., the great one amongst those sons mentioned).

(b) By placing the adjective in the construct before a definite noun, e.g., קְטֹן בָּנָיו, his youngest son (i.e., the young one of his sons).

(c) By using the preposition בְּ, "amongst", e.g., הָאִישׁ הֶחָזָק בָּאָרֶץ, the strongest man in the earth; or the comparative with כֹּל, e.g., גָּדוֹל מִכֹּל הָעָם, the greatest of all the people; or by using a pronominal suffix with an adjective, e.g., גְּדוֹלָם, their greatest (i.e., the great of them).

(d) Absolute superlatives use adverbs like מְאֹד after the adjective, e.g., גָּדוֹל עַד־מְאֹד, very great; or nouns in the construct, e.g., שִׁיר הַשִּׁירִים, the most excellent song (i.e., the song of songs).

Numerals

The numbers one to nineteen have masculine and feminine forms, whilst numbers one to ten have a construct as well as an absolute state. Numbers may be described as "cardinals" (answering the question "how many?") and "ordinals" (answering the question "in what order?"). The cardinal numbers are as follows:

	With masculine nouns		With feminine nouns	
	Abs.	Cstr.	Abs.	Cstr.
1	אֶחָד	אַחַד	אַחַת	אַחַת
2	שְׁנַיִם	שְׁנֵי	שְׁתַּיִם	שְׁתֵּי
3	שְׁלֹשָׁה	שְׁלֹשֶׁת	שָׁלֹשׁ	שְׁלֹשׁ
4	אַרְבָּעָה	אַרְבַּעַת	אַרְבַּע	אַרְבַּע
5	חֲמִשָּׁה	חֲמֵשֶׁת	חָמֵשׁ	חֲמֵשׁ
6	שִׁשָּׁה	שֵׁשֶׁת	שֵׁשׁ	שֵׁשׁ

7	שֶׁבַע	שֶׁבַע	שִׁבְעַת	שִׁבְעָה
8	שְׁמֹנֶה	שְׁמֹנֶה	שְׁמֹנַת	שְׁמֹנָה
9	תֵּשַׁע	תֵּשַׁע	תִּשְׁעַת	תִּשְׁעָה
10	עֶשֶׂר	עֶשֶׂר	עֲשֶׂרֶת	עֲשָׂרָה

11	אַחַת עֶשְׂרֵה	{ אֶחָד עָשָׂר
	עַשְׁתֵּי עֶשְׂרֵה	{ עַשְׁתֵּי עָשָׂר
12	שְׁתֵּים עֶשְׂרֵה	{ שְׁנֵים עָשָׂר
	שְׁתֵּי עֶשְׂרֵה	{ שְׁנֵי עָשָׂר
13	שְׁלֹשׁ עֶשְׂרֵה	שְׁלֹשָׁה עָשָׂר
14	אַרְבַּע עֶשְׂרֵה	אַרְבָּעָה עָשָׂר

etc.   etc.

20	עֶשְׂרִים		60	שִׁשִּׁים
30	שְׁלֹשִׁים		70	שִׁבְעִים
40	אַרְבָּעִים		80	שְׁמֹנִים
50	חֲמִשִּׁים		90	תִּשְׁעִים

100 מֵאָה (*f.*), cstr. מְאַת, plur. מֵאוֹת, hundreds.

200 מָאתַיִם (dual for מֵאתַיִם).

300 שְׁלֹשׁ מֵאוֹת 400 אַרְבַּע מֵאוֹת 500 חֲמֵשׁ מֵאוֹת etc.

1000 אֶלֶף (*m.*) 2000 אַלְפַּיִם (dual). 3000 שְׁלֹשֶׁת אֲלָפִים

4000 אַרְבַּעַת אֲלָפִים 10,000 רְבָבָה 20,000 רִבּוֹתַיִם (dual).

The numeral "one" is an adjective, and generally follows its noun, agreeing with it in gender, *e.g.*, שָׁנָה אֶחָת, one year. The number "two" is a dual form, and agrees in gender with its noun, *e.g.*, שְׁתֵּי נָשִׁים, two women. As a construct it precedes the word numbered, but as an absolute it follows it in apposition.

The cardinals from three to ten are nouns which disagree with the noun in gender, the masculine form standing with the feminine noun, and *vice versa*, e.g., שְׁלֹשֶׁת בָּנִים, three sons ; שָׁלֹשׁ בָּנוֹת, three daughters. The numerals from eleven to nineteen have the unit before the ten, and the noun is generally in the plural, though after common substantives such as day, year, man, the singular is used. The tens from thirty to ninety are expressed by the plural of the corresponding units, whilst twenty represents the plural of ten. Tens and units are usually joined by the conjunction waw, *e.g.*, שִׁבְעִים וְשִׁבְעָה, seventy-seven (*i.e.*, seventy and seven). The numerals occasionally have suffixes, as with שְׁלָשְׁתָּם, they three.

The ordinals have distinctive forms for the numbers one to ten only, as follows :

	Masculine	Feminine
first	רִאשׁוֹן	רִאשׁוֹנָה
second	שֵׁנִי	שֵׁנִית
third	שְׁלִישִׁי	שְׁלִישִׁית
fourth	רְבִיעִי	רְבִיעִית
fifth	חֲמִשִׁי	חֲמִישִׁית
sixth	שִׁשִּׁי	שִׁשִּׁית
seventh	שְׁבִיעִי	שְׁבִיעִית
eighth	שְׁמִינִי	שְׁמִינִית
ninth	תְּשִׁיעִי	תְּשִׁיעִית
tenth	עֲשִׂירִי	עֲשִׂירִית

These ordinals are adjectives, agreeing with the substantive in number and gender, and coming generally after the noun. After ten, the ordinals have no distinct form, and the corresponding cardinals are then employed. The age of people is normally expressed by בֶּן־, "son of" or בַּת, "daughter of", e.g., אִישׁ בֶּן־שְׁלֹשִׁים שָׁנָה, a man of thirty. In dates, the cardinals frequently replace ordinals in usage, e.g., בְּאֶחָד לַחֹדֶשׁ, on the first of the month.

About the Maccabean period the consonants of the alphabet came to be used as numerical signs, with the values assigned to them which we have already included in our table of the alphabet. From this it will be seen that the letters א to ט comprise the first nine numerals, the letters י to צ the tens, whilst the hundreds are signified by the letters from ק to ת. In combinations of numbers the greater symbol generally precedes the lesser, e.g., יב equals 12, i.e., 2 plus 10, the latter number being written first. Thus לג equals 3 plus 30, ריא equals 1 plus 10 plus 200, תר equals 200 plus 400, and so on. Exceptions to this are numbers 15 and 16, which are not symbolised by יה and יו respectively, since these combinations are fragments of the Divine Name. This difficulty was avoided by using טו (6 plus 9) for fifteen, and טז (7 plus 9) for sixteen.

VOCABULARY

גָּבֹהַּ	tall.	אָהַב	to love.	פֶּקַח	Pekah.
רָחֵל	Rachel.	שֵׁבֶט	tribe, sceptre.	בָּבֶל	Babylon.
לֵאָה	Leah.	שְׁלֹמֹה	Solomon.	יָדַע	to know.
חֶסֶד	kindness.	חֹדֶשׁ	month.	בָּטַח	to trust.
גָּדַל	to grow, become great.	בַּעַל	lord, master, husband.	מִלְחָמָה	battle, war (f).

Exercise 18

Translate :

1. קָטֹן מִן־אָחִיו. 2. דָּוִד הַגָּדוֹל מֵאֶחָיו. 3. בְּנוֹ הַקָּטֹן.
4. עֶבֶד עֲבָדִים. 5. אֶגְדַּל מִמְּךָ. 6. גָּבֹהַּ אָנֹכִי מִמֶּנּוּ. 7. אַחַד
שְׁבָטֶיךָ. 8. שְׁלֹשֶׁת בָּנָיו. 9. בַּחֲמִשָּׁה עָשָׂר יוֹם. 10. שְׁנַת שְׁמֹנֶה
עֶשְׂרֵה לִשְׁלֹמֹה. 11. בִּשְׁנַת שְׁתַּיִם לְפֶקַח. 12. בְּחֹדֶשׁ שְׁנַיִם
עָשָׂר בַּשָּׁנָה הַשְּׁלִישִׁית. 13. בִּשְׁנַת שְׁמֹנֶה עֶשְׂרֵה לַמֶּלֶךְ יִשְׂרָאֵל.
14. שְׁנֵיהֶם. 15. שְׁנַיִם שָׁנִים.

1. Better than gold. 2. His youngest daughter. 3. He is taller than his wife. 4. From the greatest of them to the least of them. 5. Jacob loved Rachel more than Leah. 6. I am not better than my fathers. 7. The two mountains. 8. Her three daughters. 9. Fifteen sons. 10. Sixty-two years. 11. Twenty-seven. 12. Eleven years. 13. The first earth. 14. The tenth month. 15. In the second year.

Translate from the Hebrew Bible, using a lexicon where necessary : Jeremiah 52, verses 28-32.

CHAPTER XX

VERBAL SUFFIXES

THE pronominal accusative of a verb may be expressed by את with the appropriate suffix, or by a pronominal suffix attached to the verb. Normally only a direct object is implied by the use of a verbal suffix.

The form of the suffix itself is similar to those attached to nouns, except that in the first singular נִי‎ is preferred, whilst in the third plural we find ם‎ and ו more often than הֶם—‎ and הֶן—‎. The addition of a suffix naturally affects the tone or accent, which tends to move in the direction of the suffix, and which modifies the pointing accordingly.

The inflections will be seen from the following tables:

Regular Verb

PERFECT QAL SINGULAR

	3 m.	3 f.	2 m.	2 f.	1 c.
Sing.					
1 c.	קְטָלַנִי	קְטָלַתְנִי	קְטַלְתַּנִי	קְטַלְתִּינִי	—
2 m.	קְטָלְךָ	קְטָלַתְךָ	—	—	קְטַלְתִּיךָ
2 f.	קְטָלֵךְ	קְטָלָתֶךְ	—	—	קְטַלְתִּיךְ

	3 m.	3 f.	2 m.	2 f.	1 c.
3 m.	קְטָלוֹ	קְטָלַתּוֹ	קְטָלְתּוֹ	(קְטַלְתִּיו)	קְטַלְתִּיו
	קְטָלָהוּ	קְטָלַתְהוּ	קְטַלְתָּהוּ	קְטַלְתִּיהוּ	קְטַלְתִּיהוּ
3 f.	קְטָלָהּ	קְטָלַתָּה	קְטַלְתָּהּ	קְטַלְתִּיהָ	קְטַלְתִּיהָ
Plur.					
1 c.	קְטָלָנוּ	קְטָלַתְנוּ	קְטַלְתָּנוּ	קְטַלְתִּינוּ	–
2 m.	קְטָלְכֶם	(קְטָלַתְכֶם)	–	–	קְטַלְתִּיכֶם
2 f.	קְטָלְכֶן	(קְטָלַתְכֶן)	–	–	קְטַלְתִּיכֶן
3 m.	קְטָלָם	קְטָלַתַם	קְטַלְתָּם	קְטַלְתִּים	קְטַלְתִּים
3 f.	קְטָלָן	קְטָלַתַן	קְטַלְתָּן	קְטַלְתִּין	קְטַלְתִּין

PERFECT QAL PLURAL

	3 c.	2 c.	1 c.
1 c.	קְטָלוּתִי	קְטַלְתּוּנִי	–
2 m.	קְטָלוּךָ	–	קְטַלְנוּךָ
2 f.	קְטָלוּךְ	–	קְטַלְנוּךְ
3 m.	קְטָלוּהוּ	קְטַלְתּוּהוּ	קְטַלְנוּהוּ
3 f.	קְטָלוּהָ	קְטַלְתּוּהָ	קְטַלְנוּהָ
1 c.	קְטָלוּנוּ	קְטַלְתּוּנוּ	–
2 m.	(קְטָלוּכֶם)	–	קְטַלְנוּכֶם
2 f.	(קְטָלוּכֶן)	–	קְטַלְנוּכֶן
3 m.	קְטָלוּם	קְטַלְתּוּם	קְטַלְנוּם
3 f.	קְטָלוּן	קְטַלְתּוּן	קְטַלְנוּן

The student will not encounter undue difficulty in learning these forms, as they inflect quite regularly. In the ordinary way only active verbs take suffixal forms, since the reflexives and passives cannot govern an object. Where forms are exactly alike, as with the second singular feminine and the first singular common with the third masculine suffixes, the context determines the meaning.

The Pi'el and Hiph'il follow the same general scheme, as the following two examples will indicate:

	Pi'el		Hiph'il	
	3 sg. m.	3 pl. c.	3 sg. m.	3 pl. m.
1 c.	קִטְּלַ֫נִי	קִטְּל֫וּנִי	הִקְטִילַ֫נִי	הִקְטִיל֫וּנִי
2 m.	קִטֶּלְךָ	קִטְּל֫וּךָ	הִקְטִילְךָ	הִקְטִיל֫וּךָ
2 f.	קִטְּלֵךְ	קִטְּל֫וּךְ	הִקְטִילֵךְ	הִקְטִיל֫וּךְ
3 m.	קִטְּלוֹ	קִטְּל֫וּהוּ	הִקְטִילוֹ(‏-ה֫וּ)	הִקְטִיל֫וּהוּ
3 f.	קִטְּלָהּ	קִטְּל֫וּהָ	הִקְטִילָהּ	הִקְטִיל֫וּהָ
1 c.	קִטְּלָ֫נוּ	קִטְּל֫וּנוּ	הִקְטִילָ֫נוּ	הִקְטִיל֫וּנוּ
2 m.	קִטֶּלְכֶם	קִטְּלוּכֶם	הִקְטִילְכֶם	הִיקְטִילוּכֶם
2 f.	קִטֶּלְכֶן	קִטְּלוּכֶן	הִקְטִילְכֶן	הִקְטִילוּכֶן
3 m.	קִטְּלָם	קִטְּלוּם	הִקְטִילָם	הִקְטִילוּם
3 f.	קִטְּלָן	קִטְּלוּן	הִקְטִילָן	הִקְטִילוּן

The suffix of the imperfect generally prefers an "e" vowel where the perfect has an "a" vowel. The imperfect has regular suffixal endings because the change of persons occurs with the commencing syllable. The imperfect and imperatives often have an assimilated נ, called "nun energicum" before the suffix, with dagheš forte, *e.g.*, שָׁמְרָךְ for יִשְׁמָרְנְךָ. This is common in pause.

The following tables indicate the suffixal forms found in the imperfect and imperative:

	Imperfect Qal			Imperative		
	3 sg. m.	3 sg. m. with nun energicum	3 pl.	2 sg. m.	2 sg. m. with nun energicum	2 pl. m.
1 c.	יִקְטְלֵנִי	יִקְטְלֵנִּי	יִקְטְלוּנִי	קָטְלֵנִי	קָטְלֵנִּי	קָטְלוּנִי
2 m.	יִקְטָלְךָ	יִקְטְלֶךָּ	יִקְטְלוּךָ	–	–	–
2 f.	יִקְטְלֵךְ	–	יִקְטְלוּךְ			
3 m.	יִקְטְלֵהוּ	יִקְטְלֶנּוּ	יִקְטְלוּהוּ	קָטְלֵהוּ	קָטְלֶנּוּ	קָטְלוּהוּ
3 f.	(יִקְטְלָהּ)	יִקְטְלֶנָּה	יִקְטְלוּהָ	(קָטְלָהּ)	קָטְלֶנָּה	קָטְלוּהָ
1 c.	יִקְטְלֵנוּ	יִקְטְלֶנּוּ	יִקְטְלוּנוּ	קָטְלֵנוּ	קָטְלֶנּוּ	קָטְלוּנוּ
2 m.	יִקְטָלְכֶם	–	יִקְטְלוּכֶם	–	–	–
2 f.	יִקְטָלְכֶן	–	יִקְטְלוּכֶן	–	–	–
3 m.	יִקְטְלֵם	–	יִקְטְלוּם	קָטְלֵם	–	קָטְלוּם
3 f.	יִקְטְלֵן	–	יִקְטְלֵן	קָטְלֵן	–	קָטְלֵן

	Infinitive constr.	Pi'el 3 sg. m.	Hiph'il 3 sg. m.
1 c.	קָטְלִי (קָטְלֵנִי)	יְקַטְּלֵנִי	יַקְטִילֵנִי
2 m.	קָטְלְךָ (קָטְלֶךָ)	יְקַטֶּלְךָ	יַקְטִילְךָ
2 f.	קָטְלֵךְ	יְקַטְּלֵךְ	יַקְטִילֵךְ
3 m.	קָטְלוֹ	יְקַטְּלֵהוּ	יַקְטִילֵהוּ
3 f.	קָטְלָהּ	יְקַטְּלָהּ	יַקְטִילֶהָ (יַקְטִילָהּ)

1 c.	יַקְטִילֵנוּ	יִקְטְלֵנוּ	קְטַלְנוּ
2 m.	יַקְטִילְכֶם	יִקְטְלְכֶם	קְטַלְכֶם
2 f.	יַקְטִילְכֶן	יִקְטְלְכֶן	קְטַלְכֶן
3 m.	יַקְטִילֵם	יִקְטְלֵם	קְטָלָם
3 f.	יַקְטִילֵן	יִקְטְלֵן	קְטָלָן

The student should notice that the vowel under the second masculine singular and plural of the imperfect Qal is qameç hatuph, as also in the shut syllables of the infinitive construct. The participle generally has the suffixes of the noun rather than the verb, *e.g.*, מְבַקְשָׁיו, rather than מְבַקְשֵׁהוּ, "those who seek him".

The infinitive construct has the force of a gerund, and can govern an object. Thus the phrase "when he kept the man" may be rendered בְּשָׁמְרוֹ אֶת־הָאִישׁ, with בְּ prefixed to the infinitive. If the object is a pronoun, אֵת in suffixal form is employed.

The suffixes to the verb might at first glance appear confusing and highly intricate, but with even the slightest degree of familiarity they become apparent as an ingenious method of expression involving a direct relation between subject, verb and object, and the economy of language which results is in many ways typical of the Hebrew idiom. Thus one word, שְׁמָרָתַם, means "she has kept them (*m*)", just as יַמְלִיכוּנִי does duty for the expression "they (*m.*) will make me (*c*) king". A glance at the suffix is sufficient to indicate the person of the object, whilst the state of the subject and verb is readily deduced from the remainder of the word.

VOCABULARY

בקשׁ	(Pi‘el.) to seek.	קֶדֶם	east.	מֹשֶׁה	Moses.
שׁמד	(Hiph.) to destroy.	לְמַעַן	in order that.	עוֹלָה	burnt-offering.
מָצָא	to find.	אַיֵּה	where ?	זֶרַע	seed.
רָעָב	famine.	אֵיךְ	how ?	לָשׁוֹן	tongue (f).
שָׂרַף	to burn.	רֹעֶה	shepherd.	מִנְחָה	meal-offering.
אֱמֶת	truth (f).	שָׁפַט	to judge.	בָּנָה	to build.
יָרֵא	to fear.	בָּחַר	to choose.	אַף	also, moreover.
כָּרַת בְּרִית	to make a covenant.	מָאַס	to reject, despise.	רֵעַ	friend, companion.

Exercise 19

Translate :

‎1. יְבַקְשֵׁנִי ‎2. שְׁמָרֵנוּ ‎3. יַמְלִיכֵנִי ‎4. יִשְׁמְרוּכֶן ‎5. שְׁמַרְתִּיו

‎6. שְׁמַרְתִּינִי ‎7. שְׁמָרָן ‎8. אַחֲרֵי כָּרְתָם בְּרִית ‎9. בְּקַשְׁנוּךְ

‎10. בִּקַּשְׁתָּהוּ בַבֹּקֶר ‎11. בְּשָׁמְרוּ אֶת דְּבָרֶיךָ בַּהֵיכָל

‎12. הִמְלִיכוּהוּ עַל־הָעָם הַזֶּה ‎13. מַצְדִּיקִי הוּא אֱלֹהִים

‎14. יַשְׁמִידַנִי בַּיּוֹם הַהוּא ‎15. כִּי־מְכַבְּדַי אֲכַבֵּד.

1. She has made me king (Hiph.). 2. I have kept thee.
3. They have kept them. 4. Make me king. 5. They(*m*)
will seek me. 6. Ye(*f*) have sought me. 7. We have kept
thee(*m*). 8. In thy(*f*) keeping. 9. When the man
remembered thy law. 10. In the day when I visit them.
11. He will honour me in that city. 12. I will judge thee(*f*)
according to thy ways. 13. God has sent me before you.
14. They sought him with their whole heart. 15. Hast
thou found me, O my enemy ?

Translate : Isaiah 41, verses 8-12.

CHAPTER XXI

WEAK VERBS: PE NUN, PE GUTTURAL, PE 'ALEPH

WEAK verbs are normally classified in terms of the old paradigm verb פָּעַל, which earlier grammarians regarded as the typical regular or strong verb, later being displaced in favour of קטל because of its guttural content, as we have seen. Thus, the first radical of any verb is designated the פ״ letter; the second is styled the ע״ letter, whilst the third is called the ל״ letter. On this basis פ״ן verbs are those which have נ as the first letter, and ע״ו are those which have waw as the second radical. Since א and ה are gutturals at the beginning, and quiescent letters at the end of a word, they have a twofold designation, e.g., בָּכָה is a ל״ה verb, but הָלַךְ is a פ״ guttural. Where a verb has the second and third radicals identical it is called a Double 'Ayin verb, e.g., סָבַב.

These verbs are styled "weak" because of the necessary modification of certain forms in the paradigm where the radicals are normally doubled. Since many of these radicals are gutturals, dagheš forte cannot be inserted, as in the strong or regular verb. The student should avoid the term "irregular" as far

as possible in this connection, since the form which
ensues is fully consonant with the normal procedure
governing guttural letters, already familiar to us.

Pe Nun Verbs

This type is marked by the ready assimilation of
the radical נ at the end of a syllable, since in this
position it does not carry a full vowel. This assimilation occurs in the imperfect Qal, the Niph'al perfect
and participle, and throughout the Hiph'il and
Hoph'al. Thus יִנְתֵּן becomes יִתֵּן ; נִנְתַּן becomes נִתַּן,
and so on. In this type of verb, qibbuç replaces
qameç hatuph in the Hoph'al.

The nun is dropped in the imperative by stative
verbs and those with pathah under the second
radical, e.g., גַּשׁ for נְגַשׁ, draw near. If a verb has
holem with the second radical, the nun is generally
retained, e.g., נְפֹל, fall thou. The infinite construct
relinquishes the nun, but assumes the feminine termination to form a seghoļate noun, e.g., גֶּשֶׁת. With
לְ as a prefix it is pointed with qameç, e.g., לָגֶשֶׁת, to
draw near. With a suffix this becomes לְגִשְׁתִּי, "for
my drawing near". But verbs which have holem in
the imperative form the infinitive construct in the
usual manner, retaining the nun, e.g., לִנְפֹּל to fall.

The verb לָקַח, to take, is treated as a Pe Nun verb
in the Qal and Hoph'al. Thus the Qal imperfect is

יִקַּח, and the Hoph'al imperfect is יֻקַּח. In other
formations, however, the ל is not assimilated, *e.g.*,
Niph'al, וְלִקַּח. In the verb נָתַן, to give, set, the
final nun is assimilated where pointed with silent
šᵉwa, *e.g.*, נָתַנְתְּ becomes נָתַתְּ. The initial nun is
also assimilated in the imperfect Qal and takes çere
under the second radical, *e.g.*, יִתֵּן. The imperative
likewise has çere, but before maqqeph it becomes
sᵉghol, *i.e.*, תֶּן־. The emphatic form of this is תְּנָה
and with suffix is תְּנֵהוּ. The infinitive construct is
תֵּת, from תֶּנֶת, and with a suffix is תִּתִּי, etc. With ל
the infinitive construct is לָתֵת. Fuller forms will be
found in the paradigm at the end of the book.

Pe Guttural Verbs

These verbs are modified because of the peculiar-
ities of the guttural letters. As we have seen, these
letters cannot be doubled by a dageš forte, and also
they prefer a hateph to a simple vocal šᵉwa. In the
imperfect Niph'al and related forms the initial radical
has the hireq lengthened to çere in compensation,
e.g., יֵעָמֵד. In the perfect Qal, the second plural
masculine and feminine have hateph pathah as the
guttural vowel, *i.e.*, עֲבַדְתֶּם and עֲבַדְתֶּן, where the
regular verb would have simple šᵉwa. In the imperfect the hateph occurs consistently under the
guttural, and corresponds with the vowel of the
prefix, *e.g.*, אֶעֱזֹב. Normally the vowel preferred by

the guttural is of a different class from that of the
last syllable. So in the imperfect Qal, with a final
holem the guttural vowel is generally pathah, *e.g.*,
יַעֲמֹד, and with a terminal pathah the vowel chosen
is usually sᵉghol, *e.g.*, יֶחֱזַק. However, sᵉghol is
regularly found with the first person singular of the
imperfect Qal, אֶעֱמֹד, whilst in the imperative the
hateph is usually hateph pathah, *e.g.*, עֲמֹד. Where
forms end with a vowel letter, the hateph becomes a
full vowel before a šᵉwa. Thus whilst the third
singular masculine imperfect Qal of עָמַד is יַעֲמֹד, the
third plural is יַעַמְדוּ, with the šᵉwa under the mem
being vocal. Obviously a form יַעֲמְדוּ would be impossible, since two vocal šᵉwas cannot occur together.

Pe 'Aleph Verbs

Because א is a quiescent letter as well as a guttural,
it relinquishes its consonantal force in the case of five
verbs, and these then form a subdivision of the Pe
guttural class. They are אָבַד, to perish ; אָמַר, to
say ; אָכַל, to eat ; אָפָה, to bake, and אָבָה, to be
willing. The last two are ל״ה verbs also. One or
two verbs have both Pe guttural and Pe 'Aleph forms,
e.g., אָחַז, to seize, and אָסַף, to gather.

In the perfect Qal they are like the Pe gutturals,
but in the imperfect א quiesces to the vowel holem,
e.g., יֹאכַל for יֶאֱכַל. In the infin. const. either hateph
pathah or hateph sᵉghol are found under the א, *e.g.*,

אָמַר, אָכַל. Whilst the infinitive construct when
governed or preceded by לְ normally has hateph
seghol, one verb only, אָמַר has a contracted form,
לֵאמֹר for לֶאֱמֹר. In the imperfect with waw consecutive, אָמַר has seghol, וַיֹּאמֶר *and he said*, but in the
first singular pathah is found, *e.g.*, וָאֹמַר.

VOCABULARY

נגש (Niph.) to draw near.	נצל (Hiph.) to deliver.	חֲצִי half.
נָקַם to avenge.	נבא (Niph.) to prophesy.	עָמַד to stand.
נָשַׁק to kiss.	חָטָא to sin.	שָׁכַב to sleep.
חָלַק to divide.	חָלַם to dream.	קֹדֶשׁ holiness.
דבר (Pi.) to speak.	עָנָה to answer.	יְהוֹנָתָן Jonathan.
חָכַם to be wise.	עֲנָתוֹת Anathoth.	נגע to touch, reach.
נַחֲלָה possession, inheritance (*f*).	נכה (Hiph.) to strike, kill.	עָבַד to serve, till ground.
רָחַק to be distant, withdraw.	נָטַשׁ to leave, allow.	סָפַר to count, write ; (Pi.) to recount.

Exercise 20

Translate :

‎1. וַיֹּאמֶר אֵלַי בֶּן־אָדָם עֲמֹד עַל־רַגְלֶיךָ וַאֲדַבֵּר אֹתָךְ
‎2. אֶעֱבָדְךָ שֶׁבַע שָׁנִים בְּרָחֵל .3 וְשָׁלְחוּ וְקִבְּצוּ
עִירוֹ וְלָקְחוּ אֹתוֹ מִשָּׁם וְנָתְנוּ אֹתוֹ בְּיַד־הַמֶּלֶךְ .4 כֹּה אָמַר

יהוה לַאֲשֶׁר עֲנָתוֹת הַמְבַקְשִׁים אֶת־נַפְשֶׁךָ לֵאמֹר לֹא תִנָּבֵא
בְּשֵׁם יהוה 5. וּפַרְעֹה חֹלֵם וְהִנֵּה עֹמֵד עַל־הַיְאֹר 6. וַיְדַבֵּר
יְהוֹנָתָן בְּדָוִד טוֹב אֶל־שָׁאוּל אָבִיו וַיֹּאמֶר אֵלָיו אַל־יֶחֱטָא
הַמֶּלֶךְ בְּעַבְדּוֹ 7. וְעָבַדְתָּ אֶת־אֹיְבֶיךָ אֲשֶׁר יְשַׁלְּחֵם בְּךָ יהוה
8. בְּיוֹם הָרָע אֶקְרָאֶךָּ כִּי תַעֲנֵנִי 9. לֹא נְטַשְׁתַּנִי לְנַשֵּׁק לְבָנַי
וְלִבְנֹתָי 10. וַיַּחֲלֹק עֲלֵיהֶם לַיְלָה הוּא וַעֲבָדָיו.

1. Ye(m) shall serve God upon this mountain. 2. And
thou, son of man, prophesy unto the mountains of Israel.
3. And they dreamed a dream in one night. 4. And he
said, Draw ye near hither, all the people. 5. For the place
on which you are standing (part.) is holy ground (ground
of holiness). 6. And thou shalt not cause the land to sin,
which the Lord thy God has given thee for an inheritance.
7. Thus saith Jehovah, send out (Pi'el) my people, that
they may serve me. 8. And Jehovah will answer and say
to his people, Behold I am sending(part.) bread in the desert.
9. In all these words he did not sin with his lips. 10. And
his father said unto him, draw near, I pray thee, and kiss
me, my son.

Translate : Genesis 28, verses 11-15.

CHAPTER XXII

'AYIN GUTTURAL, LAMEDH GUTTURAL AND LAMEDH 'ALEPH VERBS

'Ayin Guttural

BECAUSE the second radical in this type of verb is a guttural, certain modifications associated with gutturals take place. Thus a vocal šᵉwa under a guttural becomes a hateph, and because of the preference for "a" sounds it is usually hateph pathah, e.g., בַּחֲרוּ for בָּחְרוּ. The perfect Qal follows the normal pattern except for the third feminine singular and third plural, which have the hateph under the guttural. This occurs also in the second feminine singular, third masculine plural and second masculine plural of the imperfect, and also in the cohortative. In the feminine singular and masculine plural of the imperative the first radical takes the short vowel corresponding to the hateph, e.g., שַׁחֲטוּ instead of שְׁחֲטוּ. In both the imperfect and imperative Qal, pathah may replace holem, e.g., יִשְׁחַט rather than יִשְׁחֹט.

The Pi'el, Pu'al and Hithpa'el naturally omit dagheš forte from the middle radical, being a guttural. The preceding vowel is lengthened in com-

pensation before ר (בְּרַךְ for בְּרַךְ), and often before א
(מִאֵן for מִאֵן).   ה, ח and ע generally require no such
compensation.

Lamedh Guttural

This is a type of verb whose third radical is a
guttural, and includes final ה with mappiq. Final א
and ה simple are quiescent, and fall into different
classes to be considered later. Verbs of this general
class are peculiar because of the rule that all final
gutturals must have an "a" sound connected with
them. The imperfect and imperative Qal and
Niph'al have pathah before the guttural, whilst
pathah furtive occurs after a fully accented vowel in
the infinitives Qal and in the active participle. When
the guttural is final and preceded by a permanently
long vowel, pathah furtive is employed in the normal
manner, e.g., הִשְׁלִיחַ. An auxiliary pathah is placed
under the guttural of the second feminine singular in
the perfect Qal and elsewhere without altering the
pointing of the taw, e.g., שָׁלַחַתְּ, not שָׁלַחְתְּ.

Lamedh 'Aleph

In this class it is important to bear in mind the
quiescent nature of the final guttural, as we mentioned above. Apart from the third and second
person feminine plural of the imperfect, the preceding vowel is always long when the א quiesces, for
the syllable thus has the effect of being open.

In the perfect Qal, qameç is retained throughout, except in the stative verbs, which have çere, *i.e.*, מָצָאתָ, but מָלֵאתָ. The infinitive construct Qal may be regular, *e.g.*, חֲטֹא, but may be formed by adding ת, *e.g.*, מְלֹאת. The imperfect Qal has qameç as the second vowel, but an accented sᵉghol precedes the א in the third and second persons feminine plural, *e.g.*, תִּמְצֶאנָה.

There is a tendency to confuse forms from this class with corresponding forms of the ל״ה class of verbs, as in 1 Samuel xiv, 33, where we find חֹטְאִים for חֹטִאים. א may relinquish a vowel in contraction, *e.g.*, מֹצֵאת for מֹצֶאת, or it may drop out itself entirely in writing, *e.g.*, מָצָתִי for מָצָאתִי.

VOCABULARY

בּרך (Pi.) to bless.	מָלֵא to be full, (Pi.) to fill.	חֲנִית spear.
שׁען (Niph.) to lean.	שָׁלַח to send, let go.	חָמָס violence.
שׁבע (Niph.) to swear.	נָתַץ to break down.	שָׁחַת to be corrupt.
שָׂנֵא to hate.	מָשַׁח to anoint.	אָדוֹן lord, master.
מאן (Pi.) to refuse, be unwilling.	יָצַק to pour out.	רָעָה evil (*f*).
אִם if, whether.	מִשְׁחָה unction (*f*).	נבט to look. (Hiph.)

Exercise 21

Translate :

‎1. וַיֹּאמֶר יהוה אֶל־מֹשֶׁה כָּבֵד־לֵב פַּרְעֹה מֵאֵן לְשַׁלַּח אֶת הָעָם

‎2. וַתִּשָּׁחֵת הָאָרֶץ לִפְנֵי אֱלֹהִים וַתִּמָּלֵא הָאָרֶץ חָמָס 3. וְאַתָּה

‎תְּדַבֵּר אֶל־כָּל־חַכְמֵי־לֵב אֲשֶׁר מִלֵּאתִיו רוּחַ חָכְמָה 4. וַיְמָאֵן

‎וַיֹּאמֶר אֶל־אֵשֶׁת אֲדֹנָיו הֵן לֹא־יָדַע אֲדֹנִי וְכֹל אֲשֶׁר־יֶשׁ־לוֹ

‎נָתַן בְּיָדִי 5. וְאֵיךְ אֶעֱשֶׂה אֶת הָרָעָה הַגְּדֹלָה וְחָטָאתִי לֵאלֹהִים

‎6. וַאֲנִי שְׂנֵאתִיו כִּי לֹא יִתְנַבֵּא עָלַי טוֹב 7. וְאִם רַע בְּעֵינֵיכֶם

‎לַעֲבֹד אֶת־יהוה בַּחֲרוּ לָכֶם הַיּוֹם אֶת־מִי תַעֲבֹדוּן 8. וּזְעַקְתֶּם

‎בַּיּוֹם הַהוּא מִלִּפְנֵי מַלְכְּכֶם אֲשֶׁר בְּחַרְתֶּם לָכֶם 9. לֹא

‎יַשְׁחִיתֶךָ וְלֹא יִשְׁכַּח אֶת־בְּרִית אֲבֹתֶיךָ אֲשֶׁר נִשְׁבַּע לָהֶם

‎10. וּמָשַׁחְתָּ לִי אֵת אֲשֶׁר־אֹמַר אֵלֶיךָ.

1. And God blessed the seventh day and sanctified it.
2. He will not repent, for he is not a man, to repent. 3. He will send his messenger before thee. 4. And he sware to him concerning (‎עַל) these words. 5. And behold, Saul leaned upon his spear. 6. And the blood of thy sacrifices shall be poured upon the altar of the Lord thy God, and thou shalt eat the flesh. 7. Her poor will I satisfy with bread. 8. And he said unto Jacob, I find her not. 9. Thou shalt not hate thy brother in thine heart. 10. And thou shalt take the oil of unction and pour it upon his head and anoint him.

Translate : Genesis 6, verses 5-8.

CHAPTER XXIII

PE YODH, PE WAW; 'AYIN YODH
AND 'AYIN WAW VERBS

Pe Yodh and Pe Waw Verbs

THE majority of the Hebrew Pe Yodh verbs originally had waw as the first root letter, but since few
words ordinarily begin with waw, and in those in
which it would appear as a radical it becomes yodh,
the true difference between these types is less
apparent in the Qal than in the Niph'al and the
Hiph'il. Thus the verb יָטַב, to be good, is a genuine
Pe Yodh, whilst יָשַׁב, to sit, comes from an original
וָשַׁב, and is thus a Pe Waw. In the Hiph'il these
become הֵיטִיב, retaining the original ׳ after the ה, and
הוֹשִׁיב, with the original ׳, now quiescent, following
the ה.

The original פ״י verbs are few in number, the most
important being יָנַק, to suck, יָלַל, to howl (Hiph.),
יָטַב, to be good, and יָקַץ, to awake.

The imperfect Qal is regular, with the yodh
quiescing in the long hireq and pathah as the final
vowel, e.g., יִיטַב. The infinitive construct Qal is also
regular, יְטֹב, whilst all Hiph'il forms have çere under
the preformative ה, followed by quiescent ׳, e.g. הֵיטִיב.

A number of verbs with שׁ as their second radical are like פ״י verbs in the Qal, but in other forms are like פ״ן verbs in assimilating the first and second root letters, and using dagheš forte. These verbs are יָצַג, to place, יָצַב, to stand, יָצַת, to burn, and יָצַק, to pour. Assimilation takes place chiefly in the perfect Niph'al, and all forms of the Hiph'il and Hoph'al. Thus the Niph'al of יָצַת is נִצַּת, the Hiph'il is הִצִּית, and the Hoph'al is יֻצַּת. The verbs יָצַר, to fashion, and יָצָא, to go out, are exceptions to this procedure.

Many original פ״ו verbs surrender the consonantal force of the quiescents with many preformatives, but the Hiph'il and Hoph'al retain them to a certain extent. Thus the perfect Hiph'il of יָשַׁב is הוֹשִׁיב, and the imperfect is יוֹשִׁיב. The waw also reappears in the Niph'al, נוֹשַׁב. The imperfect Niph'al has waw with consonantal force, i.e., יִוָּשֵׁב. The first person imperfect singular has hireq rather than sᵉghol under the א. The Hoph'al הָיְשַׁב becomes הוּשַׁב.

The imperfect Qal varies somewhat in formation. In certain verbs it follows the pattern of the פ״י class, e.g., יִירָא, from יָרֵא, to fear. These include יָרֵשׁ, to inherit, יָעֵץ, to take counsel, יָעֵף, to be weary, and יָשֵׁן, to fall asleep. It will be seen that such verbs change waw to yodh in the imperfect, forming it like that of the strong stative verbs.

In other verbs the initial yodh is dropped, and a permanently long çere appears under the first consonant, with either çere as the last vowel, or pathah before a guttural. Thus יָשַׁב becomes יֵשֵׁב in the imperfect Qal, and יָדַע becomes יֵדַע. The most important of these verbs are יָשַׁב, to sit, dwell, יָרַד, to go down, יָלַד, to bear, beget, יָדַע, to know, and יָצָא, to go out. הָלַךְ, to go, is regarded also as one of these, except for the perfect and infinitive absolute Qal, and the Hithpa'el.

Adverbs

These are less developed in Hebrew than in other languages, and in addition to their derivation from nouns and pronouns may be rendered idiomatically by Hebrew verbs. Thus the perfect Hiph'il of יָטַב is employed for the adverb "well", e.g., הֵיטִיבוּ לְדַבֵּר, they have spoken well, is literally "they have 'made good' in speaking" ; the phrase "and she bore again" becomes "she added and bore", i.e., וַתּוֹסֶף לָלֶדֶת, or וַתּוֹסֶף וַתֵּלֶד (and she added to bear).

'Ayin Yodh and Waw Verbs

These classes have a quiescent yodh or waw as the middle radical, which does not appear in the perfect Qal. Thus an original קָוַם becomes קָם, and שָׂיַם becomes שָׂם. Though עו verbs are more common, both types are identical in conjugation except for the imperative, imperfect and infinitive Qal, where the original medial root letter is found as a vowel, *i.e.*, יָקוּם, יָשִׂים. In the perfect, waw is omitted through-out, whether the vowel is "a", "e", or "o", *e.g.*, בּוֹשׁ, מֵת, דָּן. The Jussives of שִׂם and קָם are יָשֵׂם and יָקֹם respectively, and when waw consecutive is added to the shortened form of the imperfect, the accent falls on the yodh, making the last syllable shut and the vowel short, *i.e.*, וַיָּ֫קָם, wayyaqom, וַיָּ֫שֶׂם, wayyasem.

A number of statives are included in this class but do not conform to any particular set pattern. Thus מוּת has a Qal perfect מֵת, מֵתָה etc., whilst בּוֹשׁ has holem instead of šureq in the Qal, בֹּשְׁתָּ, בֹּשְׁתָּ etc. In the imperfect full holem reappears, יֵבוֹשׁ, etc., as in the infinitive and active participle, בּוֹשׁ. The verb בּוֹא, to come, conjugates like קוּם, save that it has ו instead of י. Hence the imperfect is יָבוֹא, and the infinitive construct is בוֹא(לְ). שׁוּב is found in an idiomatic form meaning "to do over again". The phrase, and he arose again, would thus be rendered וַיָּ֫שָׁב וַיָּ֫קָם, *i.e.*, and he returned and arose. Some verbs have Po'lel as an intensive to replace the Pi'el, *e.g.*, קוֹמֵם (imperfect יְקוֹמֵם), and occasionally a Pilpel, כִּלְכֵּל (כוּל).

VOCABULARY

מוּת to die; (Hiph.) put to death.	בּוֹא to come; (Hiph.) to bring.	שׁוּב to return; (Hiph.) to restore.

יָטַב to be good.	יָשֵׁן to sleep.	בּוֹשׁ to be ashamed.
נַחַל stream.	נְבֵלָה corpse (f).	זַיִת olive.
נוּחַ to rest.	קוּם to arise.	יָצָא to go out.
אֵלִיָּהוּ Elijah.	שֹׁמְרוֹן Samaria.	פָּצַר בְּ to urge.

Exercise 22

Translate :

1. וַיֵּלֶךְ וַיֵּשֶׁב בַּנַּחַל אֲשֶׁר עַל־פְּנֵי הָעִיר   2. וַיָּקָם וַיֵּלֶךְ אֶל־
נַפְשׁוֹ וַיָּבֹא עַד־הַמִּדְבָּר   3. קוּם אֱכֹל כִּי רַב מִמְּךָ הַדָּרֶךְ
4. וַיֹּאמֶר יהוה אֵלָיו לֵךְ שׁוּב לְדַרְכְּךָ מִדְבָּרָה   5. וַתֹּאמֶר לָהּ
בַּת־פַּרְעֹה הוֹלִיכִי אֶת־הַיֶּלֶד הַזֶּה וְהֵינִקִהוּ   6. וַיֹּאמֶר לֹא־
יַד בְּנֵי עַמְּכֶם כִּי־אָחִיו מֵת   7. וְאַתָּה תֶּחֱזֶה מִכָּל־הָעָם
אַנְשֵׁי־חַיִל יִרְאֵי אֱלֹהִים   8. וְהַדָּגָה אֲשֶׁר בַּיְאֹר תָּמוּת   9. יֵצֵא
פַרְעֹה אֶת־רֹאשְׁךָ וַהֲשִׁיבְךָ עַל־הַהֵיכָל   10. כִּי אָנֹכִי מֵת בָּאָרֶץ
הַזֹּאת וְאַתֶּם עֹבְרִים וִירִשְׁתֶּם אֶת־הָאָרֶץ הַטּוֹבָה הַזֹּאת.

1. And he said, Go out and stand upon the mountain.
2. Go, return, for what have I done to thee? 3. And he
arose and went after Elijah. 4. And they urged him
until (עַד) he was ashamed, and he said, Send. 5. And
the king died, and he was brought to Samaria, and
they buried the king in Samaria. 6. And all the men of
valour arose and went all the night and took the corpse
of Saul. 7. And the woman took the boy and nursed (יָנַק)
him. 8. And they shall fear the name of Jehovah in the
city. 9. His seed shall inherit the earth. 10. And he
said, I will certainly return to thee in the day of evil.

Translate : 1 Kings 17, verses 10-12.

CHAPTER XXIV

DOUBLE 'AYIN, LAMEDH HE, AND
DOUBLY WEAK VERBS

DOUBLE 'Ayin verbs are very similar to the 'Ayin Waw class in many respects, exhibiting a weakness in the second and third radicals, which are identical. Some authorities think that the stems are in fact only biliteral, since the two radicals in question are frequently written as one letter, *e.g.*, קָלַל becomes קַל in the perfect Qal. Where these forms take endings, dagheš forte is used to indicate the presence of a double letter. Hence קָטְטוּ becomes קַטּוּ, and so קַטּוּ, but the dagheš is omitted in simple forms.

From this it appears that there are two forms of perfect Qal. The longer one, *e.g.*, סָבַב, is conjugated like קָטַל, but seldom appears except in the third person singular and plural. A shorter form, סַב, is much more common, and takes dagheš forte in the ב, and full holem, as will be seen from the paradigm. The longer form is transitive, the shorter one intransitive.

The imperfect Qal has two forms also, one of which reflects affinity with עו verbs. This is the most common, and using the previous verb would be יִסֹּב, with the original "a" vowel under the prefix, as in

עו verbs. With waw consecutive the accent falls on the yodh, leaving the last syllable shut, e.g., וַיָּסָב, wayyaṣobh. A resemblance to פֿן verbs is seen in the alternate form יִסֹּב, with the first radical doubled instead of the second.

The original "a" vowel occurs in the perfect Niph'al, וְנָסַב, whilst the imperfect, יִסַּב, is similar to the imperfect Qal. The Hiph'il perfect is like the Niph'al perfect except that it has two çere vowels, הֵסֵב, which appear also in the participle, מֵסֵב. Intensive forms such as the Po'el (סוֹבֵב), Pilpel (גִּלְגַּל) and Hithpalpel, (הִתְגַּלְגַּל), are sometimes found. A reduplication of the first radical, similar to that found in Aramaic, occurs in the imperfect of some verbs, e.g., יִתַּם from תָּמַם, and יִקֹּד from קָדַד.

Lamedh He verbs originally ended in yodh or waw, e.g., גָּלָה derives from an original גְּלִי, and שָׁלָה from שָׁלַו. The final ה is really a vowel-letter, since were it a consonant it would of course take mappiq, and thus bring the verb into the Lamedh guttural class.

The third masculine singular perfect in all forms terminates in ה, but otherwise the ה disappears. All imperfects terminate in ֶה in the third masculine singular, but this disappears before a vowel afformative e.g., יִגְלוּ. The original third radical, yodh, survives as a quiescent letter in the second and first persons perfect of the Qal (גָּלִיתָ, גָּלִיתִי) and Niph'al

(נִגְלֵיתָ, נִגְלֵיתִי).   The jussive is formed throughout by
dropping the הָ‍ of the imperfect by a process called
"apocopation".   Such forms are known as "apocopated forms", *i.e.*, "cut off".   Thus the jussive Qal
becomes יִגֶל, the Niph'al יִגָּל, and so on, with sᵉghol
as an auxiliary vowel where two consonants would
occur together. The cohortative הָ‍ is never attached
to ל״ה verbs ; instead the simple imperfect is employed to express the cohortative concept.

Before a mute second radical (ת, ק, כ, ד) a monosyllabic apocopation takes place, *e.g.*, וַיֵּשְׁתְּ, from שָׁתָה,
and וַיֵּבְךְ, from בָּכָה.   Pe Guttural verbs which are
also ל״ה in class will retain pathah in apocopated
forms, and so the imperfect Qal and Hiph'il of עָלָה
are יַעֲלֶה, apoc. יַעַל.   The verb רָאָה, to see, has an
imperfect יִרְאֶה, and a jussive יֵרֶא, but in the waw
consecutive the א quiesces, וַיַּרְא.   The common verb
הָיָה, to be, has its imperfect יִהְיֶה, and the jussive יְהִי,
or in pause יֶהִי.   A similar verb חָיָה, to live, is formed
in exactly the same way.

שחה, to bow down, is used in the Hithpa'lel,
reflecting the original terminal radical waw.   The
perfect is הִשְׁתַּחֲוָה (with the ת and שׁ interchangeable
by rule) ; imperfect is יִשְׁתַּחֲוֶה, and the apocopated
form is יִשְׁתַּחוּ.   Apocopation of the Hiph'il imperative
takes place chiefly in the verb רָפָה, as illustrated by
the phrase, הֶרֶף מִמֶּנִּי, let me alone.

Doubly weak verbs have more than one weak radical, as with נָשָׂא, to lift up, which is both פ"נ and ל"א. Some of the more common verbs and their principal formations are as follows :

יָצָא, to go out. imp. יֵצֵא, imperat. צֵא, Hiph. הוֹצִיא, הוֹצֵאתָ, etc. (ל"א and פ"י).

בּוֹא, to come. perf. בָּא, בָּאתָ, etc. impf. יָבוֹא, imperat. בּוֹא, Hiph. הֵבִיא, with suff. generally הֲבִיאוֹ (ל"א and ע"י).

נָשָׂא, to lift. impf. יִשָּׂא. imperat. שָׂא (with suff. שָׂאֻהוּ etc.), infin. cstr. שְׂאֵת בִּשְׂאֵת etc.). (ל"א and פ"נ)

נָגַע, to touch. impf. יִגַּע. imperat. גַּע. Hiph. perf. הִגִּיעַ, Hiph. impf. יַגִּיעַ (פ"נ and ל gt.).

Defective verbs are those which function in part only, but deficiencies may be supplemented by allied defective verbs which differ in one radical only, e.g., יָצַב and נָצַב, to place. The commonly used defective verbs are :

הָלַךְ, to go. perf. הָלַךְ. imperf. יֵלֵךְ, imperat. לֵךְ ; Hiph. הוֹלִיךְ (from ילך).

טוֹב, to be good. perf., particip. and infinitive from טוֹב (ע"י) ; impf. יִיטַב and Hiph. הֵיטִיב (from יטב).

שָׁתָה, to drink. regular in Qal ; Hiph. הִשְׁקָה, etc. (from שקה).

יָכֹל, to be able. perfect like קָטֹן, infin. cstr. יְכֹלֶת;
impf. יוּכַל (thought to be an imperfect Hophʻal,
but probably a modification of יִכַל or יוּכַל).

בּוֹשׁ, to be ashamed. perf. בּוֹשׁ, imperf. יֵבוֹשׁ, imperat.
בּוֹשׁ, Hiph. (regular) הֵבִישׁ; Hiph. also הוֹבִישׁ
(from יבשׁ).

VOCABULARY

עָלָה to go up.	בָּכָה to weep.	רָבָה to multiply.
הָרָה to conceive.	חָנַן to pity.	שָׁבָה to take captive.
סָבַב to turn, turn away.	מָאוֹר luminary.	נְשָׁמָה breath, life (f).
תֹּהוּ desolation.	יַבָּשָׁה dry land (f).	רָחַף to hover, soar.
הָיָה to be, become.	חָיָה to live.	פָּרָה to be fruitful.
קָלַל to be light, trifling; (Pi.) to curse.	כַּד earthen jar, pitcher (f).	יָתַר (Niph.) to remain.

Exercise 23

Translate :

‎1. הָאִישׁ אֲשֶׁר יְקַלֵּל אֶת־אָבִיו וְאֶת־אִמּוֹ מוֹת יוּמָת ‎2. אָרוּר
אַתָּה בְּבֹאֶךָ וְאָרוּר אַתָּה בְּצֵאתֶךָ ‎3. יִשָּׂא יהוה פָּנָיו אֵלֶיךָ וְיָשֵׂם
לְךָ שָׁלוֹם ‎4. וַתֹּאמֶר שְׁתֵה אֲדֹנִי וַתֵּרֶד כַּדָּהּ עַל־יָדָהּ בַּבְּאֵר

‫5. וַיֹּאמֶר אֱלֹהִים יְהִי אוֹר וַיְהִי־אוֹר   6. וַיְהִי־עֶרֶב וַיְהִי־בֹקֶר‬

‫8. וַיְהִי   7. כִּי־יִבְכּוּ עָלַי לֵאמֹר תְּנָה־לָּנוּ בָשָׂר   יוֹם חֲמִישִׁי‬

‫9. כִּי הִנֵּה   חָלְיוֹ חָזָק מְאֹד עַד אֲשֶׁר לֹא־נוֹתְרָה־בּוֹ נְשָׁמָה‬

‫הָעִיר אֲשֶׁר נִקְרָא שְׁמִי עָלֶיהָ אָנֹכִי מַחֵל לְהָרַע בַּיּוֹם הַזֶּה‬

‫10. וַיַּרְא אֱלֹהִים כִּי־טוֹב‬

1. And he said to her, fear not, go, do according to your word. 2. And they called on the name of their god saying, Baal, hear us, and there was no voice and no one answering them. 3. And the word of the Lord came to him saying, Arise, go to the desert. 4. And a messenger of Jehovah came to the woman and said to her, Behold, now, thou dost bear not, but thou shalt conceive a son. 5. Let there be luminaries in the firmament of the heaven. 6. Be ye fruitful and multiply and replenish the earth. 7. And he said unto Joseph, Behold, I die, but God will be with you, and will bring you again to the land of your fathers. 8. And thou shalt keep all that I am commanding thee (*part.*) to-day. 9. And he went up and looked towards the sea. 10. And the king did according to all that God commanded him.

Translate : Genesis 1, verses 1-8.

VOCABULARIES

Numbers in brackets refer to the chapters where the words in question receive their principal treatment. Declensions of nouns are indicated numerically where they might not be obvious, and nouns unmarked as to gender are masculine

ENGLISH TO HEBREW

A

Aaron, אַהֲרֹן

able, to be, יָכֹל (24)

above, up, מַעַל

Abraham, אַבְרָהָם

accusative, sign of, אֵת
(אֶת־) (12)

after, behind, אַחֲרֵי, אַחַר

age, duration, עוֹלָם

alas ! אֲהָהּ

all, כֹּל

allow, leave, to, נָטַשׁ, *Impf.*
יִטּוֹשׁ.

also, moreover, אַף

altar, מִזְבֵּחַ

among, within, בְּתוֹךְ

Anathoth, עֲנָתוֹת

and, וְ (*conj.*)

angry, to be, קָצַף

anoint, to, מָשַׁח

answer, to, עָנָה (24)

arise, stand, to, קוּם (23)

arm, an, זְרֹעַ *f.*

army, valour, force, חַיִל

ashamed, to be, בּוֹשׁ (23, 24)

ask, to, שָׁאַל

ass, an, חֲמוֹר

avenge, to, נָקַם (21)

B

Baal, lord, husband, בַּעַל

Babylon, בָּבֶל

bad, רַע

bare, to lay (lead captive)

barley, שְׂעוֹרָה *f.*

battle, war, מִלְחָמָה *f.*

be, to, become, הָיָה, *impf*
יְהִי, *apoc.* יְהִי

beasts, cattle, בְּהֵמָה *f.* 1

before, לִפְנֵי

138

begin, to, חלל, *Hiph.*
(הֵחֵל 24)

behind, (after)

behold, הִנֵּה, הֵן

between, בֵּין (*prep.*)

bind, gird, to, חָבַשׁ

bird, fowl, עוֹף 2

birthright, בְּכוֹרָה *f.*

bless, to, *Pi.* ברך

blessing, בְּרָכָה *f.*

blood, דָּם

blot out, to, (destroy)

book, סֵפֶר 2

bow, קֶשֶׁת *f.* 2

boy, יֶלֶד 2 (18) ; נַעַר 2

bread, לֶחֶם 2

break down, to, נָתַץ (22)

breath, life, נְשָׁמָה *f.*

brother, אָח (18)

build, to, בָּנָה

burn, to, שָׂרַף

burnt-offering, עוֹלָה *f.*

bury, to, קָבַר

C

cake, מָעוֹג

calf, עֵגֶל 2

captain (prince)

captive, to lead, lay bare,
גָּלָה ; take captive, שָׁבָה

capture, to, a city, לָכַד

cast, to (send)

cattle (beasts)

cease, to, leave off, חָדַל

choose, to, בָּחַר ; search
out, חָזָה (23)

city, עִיר *f.* 2

clean, to be, become pure,
טָהַר ; *Pi.* to cleanse

collect, gather, to, קָשַׁשׁ

come, to בּוֹא ; *Hiph.*
(הֵבִיא), to bring (23, 24)

command, to, *Pi.* צוה (24)

command, a, מִצְוָה *f.* 1

companion (friend)

corpse, נְבֵלָה *f.*

corrupted, to be (destroy)

couch, עֶרֶשׂ *f.* 2

counsel, עֵצָה *f.*

count, write, to, סָפַר ; *Pi.*
to recount

courage, to take, (strong)

covenant, בְּרִית *f.* 2

cover, to, *Pi.* כסה

create, fashion, to, בָּרָא

cross, pass over, to, עָבַר (21)

cry, call, to, קָרָא ; cry out, זָעַק

curse, to, אָרַר (24) ; *Pi.* קִלֵּל

cut off, cut down, to, כָּרַת

D

darkness, חֹשֶׁךְ 2

daughter, בַּת *f.* 2 (18)

David, דָּוִד, דָּוִיד

day, יוֹם 2 (18)

dead, מֵת

death, put to, kill, to מוּת (23)

deliver, to, *Hiph.* נצל (הִצִּיל) (21)

desert, מִדְבָּר

desolation, תֹּהוּ

despise, reject, to, מָאַס

destroy, blot out, to, מָחָה ; *Hiph.* שָׁמַד ; to be corrupted, שָׁחַת

dig, to, כָּרָה

disease, sickness, חֳלִי 2

distant, to be, withdraw, to, רָחַק

divide, to, חָלַק ; *Hiph.* בדל

do, make, to, עָשָׂה ; פָּעַל (*poet.*) (22)

door, דֶּלֶת *f.* 2

dove, יוֹנָה *f.* (9)

draw near, to, נגשׁ, *impf. only in Qal; Niph.* to draw near (21)

dream, to, חָלַם (21)

dream, a, חֲלוֹם

drink, to, שָׁתָה

dry land, יַבָּשָׁה *f.* 1

duration (age)

dust, עָפָר 1

dwell, sit, to, יָשַׁב ; שָׁכַן

E

ear, אֹזֶן *f.* 2

earth, land, אֶרֶץ *f.* 2, *pl.* אֲרָצוֹת

earthen jar (pitcher)

east, קֶדֶם

eat, to, אָכַל

Egypt, מִצְרַיִם

Elijah, אֵלִיָּהוּ

enemy, אֹיֵב 3

evening, עֶרֶב 2

ever, for, עַד־עוֹלָם

evil, to do, *Hiph.* רעע

evil, רָעָה *f.* 2 ; רָשָׁע (*adj.*)

except, כִּי אִם

eye, עַיִן *f.* 2

F

face, פָּנִים 1

fall, to, נָפַל (21)

fashion, to, (create)

father, אָב (18)

fear, to, יָרֵא, *impf.* יִירָא (23)

few, a, little, מְעַט

fight, to, *Niph.* לחם

fig tree, תְּאֵנָה *f.*

find, to, מָצָא (22)

fire, אֵשׁ *f.* 2

firmament, רָקִיעַ 1

firstborn, בְּכוֹר

fish, a, דָּג 1

flesh, בָּשָׂר

food, אָכְלָה 2 (*f.* 2) אֹכֶל

foot, רֶגֶל *f.* 2

force (army)

forget, to, שָׁכַח

four, אַרְבַּע (19)

fowl (bird)

friend, רֵעַ (רֵעָה)

fruitful, to be, פָּרָה (24)

full, to be, מָלֵא ; *Pi.* to fill

G

garden, גַּן 2

gate, opening, פֶּתַח

gather, to, אָסַף, *impf.* יֶאֱסֹף ;
קָבַץ ; collect, קָשַׁשׁ

gird, bind, to, חָבַשׁ

girl, נַעֲרָה *f.* 2

give, set, to, נָתַן (21)

glory, כָּבוֹד

go, to, הָלַךְ ; *Hith.* to walk
(24) ; go down, יָרַד ; go
out, יָצָא, *impf.* יֵצֵא (23,
24) ; go up, עָלָה, *impf.*
יַעֲלֶה *apoc.* יַעַל

God, אֱלֹהִים

gold, זָהָב

good, to be, יָטַב (23)

good, טוֹב

goodness, טוֹבָה *f.*

good things, goodness, טוּב

grave, קֶבֶר 2

great, to be, grow, גָּדַל ; *Pi.*
to magnify

great, גָּדוֹל ; great, much,
רַב

greatness, גֹּדֶל

grievous (strong)

ground, אֲדָמָה *f.* 1

guilty, רָשָׁע

H

half, חֲצִי

hand, יָד f. 1

handmaid, שִׁפְחָה f.

hate, to, שָׂנֵא (22)

head, ראֹשׁ

health (peace)

hear, to, שָׁמַע

heart, 1 לֵבָב, 2 לֵב

heaven, שָׁמַיִם 1

heavy, to be, כָּבֵד ; Pi. to
harden, honour ; Hiph. be
honoured

hero, mighty man, גִּבּוֹר

hide, to, Pi. and Hiph.
סתר

high, lofty, רָם

hill, mountain, 2 הַר

hither, הֲלֹם

holiness, קֹדֶשׁ

holy, to be, קָדֵשׁ ; Pi. to
hallow, sanctify

holy, קָדוֹשׁ

horn, קֶרֶן f. 2

horse, סוּס 2

house, בַּיִת 2 (18)

hover, to, רָחַף

how ? how ! מָה, אֵיךְ

how much ? כַּמָּה

husband (Baal)

I

I, אֲנִי (10)

if, whether, אִם

image, likeness, צֶלֶם 2

inherit, possess, to יָרַשׁ ;
Hiph. (הוֹרִישׁ), to dis-
possess

inheritance (possession)

iniquity (sin)

in order than, לְמַעַן (prep.)

Isaac, יִצְחָק

Israel, יִשְׂרָאֵל

is, there, are, was, were, שֵׁ
יֵשׁ־

J

Jacob, יַעֲקֹב

Jehovah, יהוה

Jonathan, יְהוֹנָתָן

Joseph, יוֹסֵף

Joshua, יְהוֹשֻׁעַ, יְהוֹשׁוּעַ

Judah, יְהוּדָה

judge, to, שָׁפַט

justice, ordinance, מִשְׁפָּט

K

keep, to, שָׁמַר

kill, slay, to, הָרַג ;   put to death, מוּת (23) ;   kill smite, *Hiph.* נכה (הִכָּה), *impf. apoc.* יַךְ (21, 24)

kindness (mercy)

king, to be, מָלַךְ ;   *Hiph.* to make king

king, מֶלֶךְ 2

kiss, to, נָשַׁק (with לְ of persons)

knee, בֶּרֶךְ *f.* 2, dual בִּרְכַּיִם

know, to, יָדַע·

L

land (earth)

law, תּוֹרָה *f.*

lead captive, to, lay bare, to, (captive)

Leah, לֵאָה

lean, to, *Niph.* שׁען

leave, to, (allow)

leave off, to, (cease)

lest, פֶּן־

let go, to (send)

lie down, to (sleep)

life (breath)

lift up, to, נָשָׂא (22, 24)

light, insignificant, to be, קָלַל ;   *Pi.* to curse (24)

light, אוֹר 2

likeness (image)

lion, אֲרִי 2

lip, שָׂפָה *f.*

little, a, (few)

live, to, חָיָה (24)

living, חַי

lofty (high)

look, to, *Hiph.* נבט (הִבִּיט) (22)

lord (Baal) ;   lord, master, אָדוֹן 1

love, to, אָהַב. *impf.* יֶאֱהַב

luminary, מָאוֹר

M

magnify, to, (great)

make, do, to, עָשָׂה

male, זָכָר 1

man, mankind, אָדָם ;   man. אִישׁ

master (lord)

meal-offering, מִנְחָה *f.* 2

mercy, kindness, חֶסֶד 2

messenger, מַלְאָךְ

middle, תָּוֶךְ

mighty man (hero)

month, חֹדֶשׁ 2

moreover (also)

morning, בֹּקֶר 2

Moses, מֹשֶׁה

mother, אֵם f. 2

mountain (hill)

much (great)

multiply, to, רָבָה

N

name, שֵׁם 3

new, חָדָשׁ 1

night, לַיְלָה 2, pl. לֵילוֹת

no, none, אַיִן; no, not, אַל־ (with prohib.); not, לֹא

north, צָפוֹן f. 1

now, shortly, עַתָּה

number, מִסְפָּר

O

oil, שֶׁמֶן

old, old man, זָקֵן

old age, זְקֻנִים (זִקְנָה f.)

old, from of, מֵעוֹלָם

olive, זַיִת

one, אֶחָד (19)

opening (gate)

ordinance (justice)

over, upon, עַל־ (prep.)

ox, שׁוֹר

P

palace (temple)

pass over, to, (cross)

peace, health, שָׁלוֹם

Pekah, פֶּקַח

people, עַם 2

perfect, תָּמִים

Pharaoh, פַּרְעֹה

piece, a, פַּת f.

pitcher, earthen jar, כַּד f.

pity, to, חָנַן

place, set, to, שִׂים, שׂוֹם (23)

place, a, מָקוֹם

poor, אֶבְיוֹן 1

possess, to (inherit)

possession, inheritance, נַחֲלָה f.

pour out, to, יָצַק

powerful, עָצוּם

prayer, תְּפִלָּה f.

priest, כֹּהֵן 3

prince, captain, שַׂר

prison, ‏כְּלוּא (כֶּלֶא)‎

promise, to, (say)

prophesy, to, *Niph.* ‏נבא‎

prophet, ‏נָבִיא‎ I

pursue, to, ‏רָדַף‎

Q

queen, ‏מַלְכָּה‎ *f.* 2

R

Rachel, ‏רָחֵל‎

reach, touch, to, ‏נָגַע‎ (24)

refuse, be unwilling, to, *Pi.* ‏מאן‎

reject, to, (despise)

remain, to, *Niph.* ‏יתר‎

remember, to ‏זָכַר‎ ; *Hiph.* to bring to remembrance

repent, to, *Niph.* ‏נחם‎ (22)

rest, to, ‏נוּחַ‎ (23) ; ‏שָׁבַת‎

return, to, ‏שׁוּב‎ (23)

righteousness, ‏צֶדֶק‎ 2

river, ‏נָהָר‎ ; ‏יְאֹר‎ (of Nile)

rule, to, ‏מָשַׁל‎ (over, ‏בְּ‎)

S

sacrifice, slaughter, to, ‏זָבַח‎

sacrifice, a, ‏זֶבַח‎

Samaria, ‏שֹׁמְרוֹן‎

Samuel, ‏שְׁמוּאֵל‎

sanctify, to, (holy)

satisfied, to be, ‏שָׂבַע‎ ; *Hiph.* to satisfy

Saul, ‏שָׁאוּל‎

say, to, promise, ‏אָמַר‎ (21)

saying (word)

sceptre, tribe, ‏שֵׁבֶט‎

sea, ‏יָם‎ 2

search out, to, (choose)

see, to, ‏רָאָה‎

seed, ‏זֶרַע‎ 2

seek, to, *Pi.* ‏בקשׁ‎

sell, to, ‏מָכַר‎

send, let go, to, ‏שָׁלַח‎

seraph, ‏שָׂרָף‎ I

servant, slave, ‏עֶבֶד‎ 2

serve, till the ground, to, ‏עָבַד‎ (21)

set, to (give) ; (place)

shed, to, ‏שָׁפַךְ‎

shepherd, ‏רֹעֶה‎

short, ‏קָצֵר‎

shortly (now)

sickness (disease)

side, ‏יַרְכָּה‎ *f.* 2

sign, אוֹת

silver, כֶּסֶף 2

sin, to, חָטָא (21)

sin, iniquity, עָוֹן 1

sit, to (dwell)

skin, עוֹר

slay, to (kill)

sleep, to, יָשֵׁן, *Impf.* יִישַׁן;
lie down, שָׁכַב

smite, to (kill)

soar (hover)

Solomon, שְׁלֹמֹה

son, בֵּן 3 (18)

song, שִׁיר

soul, life, נֶפֶשׁ *f.* 2

south, נֶגֶב

speak, to, *Pi.* דבר

spear, חֲנִית *f.*

spirit (wind)

staff, מַקֵּל

stand, to, עָמַד; *Hiph.* to
place, set (21); (arise)

steal, to, גּנב

stone, אֶבֶן *f.* 2 (18)

stream, torrent, נַחַל 2

strong, to be, חָזַק; *Hith.* to
take courage; אָמַץ; *Pi.*
to strengthen

strong, grievous, חָזָק

sun, שֶׁמֶשׁ

swear, to, *Niph.* שבע

sword, חֶרֶב *f.* 2

T

table, שֻׁלְחָן

take, to, לָקַח

tall, גָּבֹהַּ

temple, palace, הֵיכָל

terebinth, אֵלָה *f.*

thence, מִשָּׁם

there, שָׁם

thing (word)

this, זֶה (10)

thither, שָׁמָּה

throne, seat, כִּסֵּא

thus, כֹּה

till the ground, to (serve)

tomorrow, מָחָר

tongs (dual) מֶלְקָחַיִם

tongue, לָשׁוֹן *f.* 1

torrent (stream)

touch, to; (reach)

towards (unto)

tree, twig, עֵץ 1

tribe (sceptre)

trumpet, שׁוֹפָר

trust, to, בָּטַח

truth, אֱמֶת f. 2

turn, turn away, to, סָבַב (24)

U

unction, מִשְׁחָה f.

under, תַּחַת

until, unto, ־עַד (prep.)

unto, towards, ־אֶל (prep.)

unwilling, to be, (refuse)

up (above)

upon (over)

upright, יָשָׁר

urge, to, בְּ פָּצַר

V

valour (army)

vengeance, נְקָמָה f. 1

very, מְאֹד ; very good, טוֹב מְאֹד

vineyard, כֶּרֶם 2

violence, חָמָס 1

visit, to, פָּקַד

voice, קוֹל 2

W

walk, to, (go)

war (battle)

water(s) מַיִם

way, דֶּרֶךְ 2

weep, to, בָּכָה

well, בְּאֵר f. 2

wheat, חִטָּה f. (9)

where ? אַיֵּה

wherein ? בַּמֶּה

whether (if)

who, which, אֲשֶׁר (10)

why ? לָמָּה

widow, אַלְמָנָה f.

wind, spirit, רוּחַ

wisdom, חָכְמָה f. 2

wise, to be, חָכַם

wise, חָכָם

with, אֵת (prep.).

withdraw, to, (be distant)

within (among)

woman, אִשָּׁה f.

word, thing, דָּבָר ; saying, מִלָּה f.

write, to, כָּתַב

Y

year, שָׁנָה f.

youth, עֲלוּמִים

HEBREW TO ENGLISH

'Aleph

אָב father (18)

אֶבְיוֹן poor

אֶבֶן stone *f.* 2 (18)

אַבְרָהָם Abraham

אָדָם man, mankind

אֲדָמָה ground *f.* 1

אָדוֹן lord, master

אָהַב to love, *impf.* יֶאֱהַב

אֲהָהּ alas!

אַהֲרֹן Aaron

אוֹר light 2

אוֹת sign

אֹזֶן ear *f.* 2

אָח brother (18)

אֶחָד one (19)

אַחֲרֵי, אַחַר after, behind

אֹיֵב enemy 3

אַיֵּה where ?

אֵיךְ how ? how!

אַיִן no, none

אִישׁ man

אִשָּׁה woman *f.*

אָכַל to eat

אֹכֶל food 2 (אָכְלָה *f.* 2)

אַל־ no, not

אֶל (*prep.*) unto,
     towards

אֵלָה terebinth *f.*

אֱלֹהִים God (*pl.*)

אֵלִיָּהוּ Elijah

אַלְמָנָה widow *f.*

אִם if, whether

אֵם mother *f.* 2

אָמַץ to be strong ; *pi.*
     to strengthen

אָמַר to say, promise
     (21)

אֱמֶת truth *f.* 2

אֲנִי I (10)

אָסַף to gather, *impf.*
     יֶאֱסֹף

אַף also, moreover

אַרְבַּע four (19)

אֲרִי lion 2

אֶרֶץ earth, land *f.* 2
     (*pl.* אֲרָצוֹת)

אָרַר to curse (24)

אֵשׁ fire *f.* 2

אֲשֶׁר who, which (10)

אֵת (אֶת־) sign of accus. (12)

אֵת (*prep*.) with

Beth

בְּאֵר well *f.* 2

בָּבֶל Babylon

בדל *Hiph*. to divide

בְּהֵמָה beasts, cattle *f.* 1

בּוֹא to come; *Hiph*. (הֵבִיא) to bring (23, 24)

בּוֹשׁ to be ashamed (23, 24)

בָּחַר to choose

בָּטַח to trust

בֵּין (*prep*.) between

בַּיִת house 2 (18)

בָּכָה to weep

בְּכוֹר firstborn

בְּכוֹרָה birthright *f.* 1

בַּמֶּה wherein?

בֵּן son 3 (18)

בָּנָה to build

בַּעַל lord, husband, Baal

בֹּקֶר morning 2

בקשׁ *Pi*. to seek

בָּרָא to create, fashion

בְּרִית covenant *f.*

בֶּרֶךְ knee *f.* 2 (dual בִּרְכַּיִם)

ברך *Pi*. to bless

בְּרָכָה blessing

בָּשָׂר flesh

בַּת daughter *f.* 2 (18)

בְּתוֹךְ within, among

Gimel

גָּבֹהַּ tall

גִּבּוֹר hero, mighty man

גָּדַל to be great, grow; *Pi*. to magnify

גֹּדֶל greatness

גָּדוֹל great

גָּלָה to lay bare, *Hiph*. to lead captive

גָּנַב to steal

Daleth

דבר *Pi*. to speak

דָּבָר word, thing

דָּג a fish

דָּוִיד, דָּוִד David

דֶּלֶת door *f.* 2

דָּם blood

דֶּרֶךְ way 2

He

הוּא, הִיא pronoun (10)

הָיָה to be, become,
Impf. יִהְיֶה, apoc.
יְהִי

הֵיכָל temple, palace

הָלַךְ to go; Hith. to
walk (24)

הֲלֹם hither

הִנֵּה הֵן behold

הַר mountain, hill 2

הָרַג to kill, slay

Waw

וְ (conj.) and

Zayin

זָבַח to sacrifice,
slaughter

זֶבַח a sacrifice 2

זֶה this (10)

זָהָב gold

זַיִת olive 2

זָכַר to remember;
Hiph. to bring
to remembrance

זָכָר male

זָעַק to cry out

זָקֵן old, old man

זְקֵנִים old age (זִקְנָה f.)

זְרוֹעַ an arm f.

זֶרַע seed

Heth

חבא Hith. to hide
oneself

חָבַשׁ to bind, gird

חָדַל to cease, leave off

חָדָשׁ new

חֹדֶשׁ month 2

חָזָה to search out,
choose (23)

חָזַק to be strong;
Hith. to take
courage

חָזָק strong, grievous

חָטָא to sin (21)

חִטָּה wheat f. (9)

חָיָה to live (24)

חַי living

חַיִּים life

חַיִל force, army, valour

חָכַם to be wise

חָכָם wise

חָכְמָה wisdom f. 2

חֳלִי disease, sickness 2

חָלַל *Hiph.* (הֵחֵל) to begin (24)

חָלַם to dream (21)

חֲלוֹם a dream

חָלַק to divide

חֲמוֹר an ass

חָמָס violence

חֲנִית spear *f.*

חָנַן to pity

חֶסֶד kindness, mercy 2

חֲצִי half

חֶרֶב sword *f.* 2

חֹשֶׁךְ darkness 2

Teth

טָהֵר to be clean, become pure ; *Pi.* to cleanse

טוֹב good

טוּב good things, goodness

טוֹבָה goodness *f.*

Yodh

יְאֹר river

יַבָּשָׁה dry land *f.* 1

יָד hand *f.* 1

יָדַע to know

יְהוּדָה Judah

יהוה Jehovah

יְהוֹנָתָן Jonathan

יְהוֹשֻׁעַ, יְהוֹשׁוּעַ Joshua

יוֹם day 2 (18)

יוֹנָה dove *f.* (9)

יוֹסֵף Joseph

יָטַב to be good (23)

יָכֹל to be able (24)

יֶלֶד boy 2 (18)

יָם sea 2

יַעֲקֹב Jacob

יָצָא to go out, *Impf.* יֵצֵא (23, 24)

יִצְחָק Isaac

יָצַק to pour out

יָרֵא to fear, *Impf.* יִירָא (23)

יָרַד to go down

יַרְכָּה side *f.* 2

יָרַשׁ to inherit, possess ; *Hiph.* (הוֹרִישׁ) to dispossess

יֵשׁ, יֶשׁ־ there is, are, was, were

יָשַׁב to sit, dwell

יָשֵׁן to sleep, *Impf* יִישָׁן

יָשָׁר upright

יִשְׂרָאֵל   Israel

יתר   *Niph.* to remain

Kaph

כָּבֵד   to be heavy ; *Pi.*
to harden,
honour ; *Niph.*
to be honoured

כָּבוֹד   glory

כַּד   earthen jar,
pitcher *f.*

כֹּה   thus

כֹּהֵן   priest 3

כִּי אִם   except

כֶּלֶא   prison

כֹּל   all

כַּמָּה   how much ?

כִּסֵּא   seat, throne

כסה   *Pi.* to cover

כֶּסֶף   silver 2

כָּרָה   to dig

כֶּרֶם   vineyard 2

כָּרַת   to cut off, down

כָּתַב   to write

Lamedh

לֹא   not

לֵאָה   Leah

לֵב, לֵבָב   heart 2

לחם   *Niph.* to fight

לֶחֶם   bread 2

לַיְלָה   night 2 (*pl.* לֵילוֹת)

לָכַד   to capture (city)

לָמָּה   why ?

לְמַעַן   (*prep.*) in order that

לִפְנֵי   before

לָקַח   to take

לָשׁוֹן   tongue *f.*

Mem

טוֹב מְאֹד   very ; very good

מָאוֹר   luminary

מאן   *Pi.* to be unwilling,
refuse

מָאַס   to reject, despise

מִדְבָּר   desert

מות   *Hiph.* to kill, put to
death (23)

מִזְבֵּחַ   altar 3

מָחָה   to destroy, blot out

מָחָר   tomorrow

מַיִם   waters

מָכַר   to sell

מָלֵא   to be full ; *Pi.* to
fill

מַלְאָךְ messenger

מִלָּה saying, word *f.*

מִלְחָמָה battle, war *f.*

מָלַךְ to be king ; *Hiph.*
to make king

מֶלֶךְ king 2

מַלְכָּה queen *f.* 2

מֶלְקָחַיִם tongs (dual)

מִנְחָה meal offering *f.* 2

מִסְפָּר number

מָעוֹג cake

מֵעוֹלָם from of old

מְעַט a little, few

מֵעַל above, up

מָצָא to find (22)

מִצְוָה command *f.*

מִצְרַיִם Egypt

מָקוֹם place

מַקֵּל staff

מֹשֶׁה Moses

מָשַׁח to anoint

מִשְׁחָה unction *f.*

מָשַׁל (בְּ) to rule (over)

מִשָּׁם thence

מִשְׁפָּט ordinance, justice

מֵת dead

Nun

נבא *Niph.* to prophesy

נָבִיא prophet 1

נבט *Hiph.* (הִבִּיט) to
look (22)

נְבֵלָה corpse *f.*

נֶגֶב south

נָגַע to touch, reach (24)

נגשׁ *only Impf. in Qal.*
(יִגַּשׁ) ; *Niph.* to
draw near (21)

נָהָר river

נוּחַ to rest (23)

נַחַל torrent, stream 2

נַחֲלָה inheritance,
possession

נחם *Niph.* to repent
(22)

נָטַשׁ to leave, allow,
Impf. יִטֹּשׁ

נָכָה *Hiph.* (הִכָּה) to
smite, kill, *Impf.*
apoc. יַךְ (21, 24)

נַעַר lad 2

נַעֲרָה girl *f.* 2

נָפַל to fall (21)

נֶפֶשׁ soul, life *f.* 2

נצל *Hiph.* (הִצִּיל) to deliver (21)

נָקַם to avenge (21)

נְקָמָה vengeance *f.*

נְשָׁמָה breath, life *f.*

נָשַׁק to kiss (with לְ of persons) (21)

נָשָׂא to lift up (22, 24)

נָתַן to give, set (21)

נָתַץ to break down (22)

Samekh

סָבַב to turn, turn away (24)

סוּס horse 2

סָפַר to count, write; *Pi.* to recount

סֵפֶר book 2

סתר *Pf.* and *Hiph.* to hide

Ayin

עָבַד to serve, till the ground (21)

עֶבֶד servant, slave 2

עָבַר to pass over, cross (21)

עֵגֶל calf 2

עַד־ (*prep.*) until, unto

עוֹלָה burnt offering *f.*

עוֹלָם age, duration (עַד־עוֹלָם, for ever)

עָוֹן sin, iniquity 1

עוֹף fowl, bird 2

עוֹר skin

עַיִן eye *f.* 2

עִיר city *f.* 2

עַל־ (*prep.*) upon, over

עָלָה to go up, *Impf.* יַעֲלֶה *apoc.* יַעַל (24)

עֲלוּמִים youth

עַם people 2

עָמַד to stand; *Hiph.* to place, set (21)

עָנָה to answer (24)

עֲנָתוֹת Anathoth

עָפָר dust 1

עֵץ tree, twig 1

עֵצָה counsel *f.*

עָצוּם powerful

עֶרֶב evening 2

עֶרֶשׂ couch *f.* 2

עָשָׂה to do, make

עַתָּה now, shortly

Pe

פֶּן־ lest

פָּנִים face (*pl.*)

פָּעַל to do (22)

פָּצַר בְּ to urge

פָּקַד to visit

פֶּקַח Pekah

פָּרָה to be fruitful (24)

פַּרְעֹה Pharaoh

פַּת a piece

פֶּתַח opening, gate

Çadhe

צֶדֶק righteousness 2

צוה *Pi.* to command (24)

צֶלֶם image, likeness 2

צָפוֹן north *f.* 1

Qoph

קָבַץ to gather

קָבַר to bury

קֶבֶר grave 2

קֹדֶשׁ holy

קֶדֶם east

קָדַשׁ to be holy ; *Pi.* to hallow, sanctify

קֹדֶשׁ holiness 2

קוֹל voice 2

קוּם to arise, stand (23)

קָלַל to be light, insignificant ; *Pi.* to curse (24)

קָצַף to be angry

קָצֵר short

קָרָא to call cry

קָרַב to draw near

קֶרֶן horn *f.* 2

קָשַׁשׁ to gather, collect

קֶשֶׁת bow *f.* 2

Resh

רָאָה to see

רֹאשׁ head

רַב great, much

רָבָה to multiply

רֶגֶל foot *f.* 2

רָדַף to pursue

רוּחַ wind, spirit *f.*

רעע *Hiph.* to do evil

רָחֵל Rachel

רָחַף to hover, soar

רָחַק to be distant, withdraw

רָם high

רַע bad

רֵעַ friend, companion

רָעָב famine

רָעָה evil *f.*

רֹעֶה shepherd

רָקִיעַ firmament

רָשָׁע wicked, guilty, evil

Sin

שָׂבַע to be satisfied ;
  Hiph. to satisfy

שִׂים, שָׂם to place, set (23)

שָׂנֵא to hate (22)

שְׂעוֹרָה barley *f.*

שָׂפָה lip *f.*

שַׂר prince, captain

שָׂרַף to burn

שָׂרָף seraph

Sin

שָׁאוּל Saul

שָׁאַל to ask

שָׁבָה to take captive

שֵׁבֶט tribe, sceptre

שבע *Niph.* to swear

שָׁבַת to rest

שׁוּב to return

שׁוֹפָר trumpet

שׁוֹר ox

שָׁחַת to destroy, be
  corrupted

שִׁיר song

שָׁכַב to sleep, lie down

שָׁכַח to forget

שָׁכַן to dwell

שָׁלוֹם peace, health

שָׁלַח to send, let go

שֻׁלְחָן table

שְׁלֹמֹה Solomon

שָׁם there

שֵׁם name

שמד *Hiph.* to destroy

שָׁמָּה thither

שְׁמוּאֵל Samuel

שָׁמַיִם heaven (*pl.*)

שֶׁמֶן oil

שָׁמַע to hear

שָׁמַר to keep

שֹׁמְרוֹן Samaria

שֶׁמֶשׁ sun

שָׁנָה year

שָׁעַן *Niph.* to lean

שִׁפְחָה handmaid *f.*

שָׁפַט to judge

שָׁפַךְ to shed

שָׁתָה to drink

Taw

תְּאֵנָה fig tree *f.*

תֹּהוּ desolation

תָּוֶךְ middle

תּוֹרָה law *f.*

תַּחַת under

תָּמִים perfect

תְּפִלָּה prayer *f.*

PARADIGMS

THE REGULAR VERB

	Qal Active	Qal Stative		Niph'al
Perfect.				
Sing. 3 m.	קָטַל	כָּבֵד	קָטֹן	נִקְטַל
3 f.	קָטְלָה	כָּבְדָה	קָטְנָה	נִקְטְלָה
2 m.	קָטַלְתָּ	כָּבַדְתָּ	קָטֹנְתָּ	נִקְטַלְתָּ
2 f.	קָטַלְתְּ	כָּבַדְתְּ	קָטֹנְתְּ	נִקְטַלְתְּ
1 c.	קָטַלְתִּי	כָּבַדְתִּי	קָטֹנְתִּי	נִקְטַלְתִּי
Plur. 3 c.	קָטְלוּ	כָּבְדוּ	קָטְנוּ	נִקְטְלוּ
2 m.	קְטַלְתֶּם	כְּבַדְתֶּם	קְטָנְתֶּם	נִקְטַלְתֶּם
2 f.	קְטַלְתֶּן	כְּבַדְתֶּן	קְטָנְתֶּן	נִקְטַלְתֶּן
1 c.	קָטַלְנוּ	כָּבַדְנוּ	קָטֹנּוּ	נִקְטַלְנוּ
Imperfect.				
Sing. 3 m.	יִקְטֹל	יִכְבַּד	יִקְטַן	יִקָּטֵל
3 f.	תִּקְטֹל	תִּכְבַּד	etc.	תִּקָּטֵל
2 m.	תִּקְטֹל	תִּכְבַּד		תִּקָּטֵל
2 f.	תִּקְטְלִי	תִּכְבְּדִי		תִּקָּטְלִי
1 c.	אֶקְטֹל	אֶכְבַּד		אִקָּטֵל¹
Plur. 3 m.	יִקְטְלוּ	יִכְבְּדוּ		יִקָּטְלוּ
3 f.	תִּקְטֹלְנָה	תִּכְבַּדְנָה		תִּקָּטַלְנָה
2 m.	תִּקְטְלוּ	תִּכְבְּדוּ		תִּקָּטְלוּ
2 f.	תִּקְטֹלְנָה	תִּכְבַּדְנָה		תִּקָּטַלְנָה
1 c.	נִקְטֹל	נִכְבַּד		נִקָּטֵל

1. or אֶקָּטֵל

The Regular Verb

Pi'el	Pu'al	Hiph'il	Hoph'al	Hithpa'el
² קִטֵּל	קֻטַּל	הִקְטִיל	הָקְטַל	הִתְקַטֵּל ı
קִטְּלָה	קֻטְּלָה	הִקְטִילָה	הָקְטְלָה	הִתְקַטְּלָה
קִטַּלְתָּ	קֻטַּלְתָּ	הִקְטַלְתָּ	הָקְטַלְתָּ	הִתְקַטַּלְתָּ
קִטַּלְתְּ	קֻטַּלְתְּ	הִקְטַלְתְּ	הָקְטַלְתְּ	הִתְקַטַּלְתְּ
קִטַּלְתִּי	קֻטַּלְתִּי	הִקְטַלְתִּי	הָקְטַלְתִּי	הִתְקַטַּלְתִּי
קִטְּלוּ	קֻטְּלוּ	הִקְטִילוּ	הָקְטְלוּ	הִתְקַטְּלוּ
קִטַּלְתֶּם	קֻטַּלְתֶּם	הִקְטַלְתֶּם	הָקְטַלְתֶּם	הִתְקַטַּלְתֶּם
קִטַּלְתֶּן	קֻטַּלְתֶּן	הִקְטַלְתֶּן	הָקְטַלְתֶּן	הִתְקַטַּלְתֶּן
קִטַּלְנוּ	קֻטַּלְנוּ	הִקְטַלְנוּ	הָקְטַלְנוּ	הִתְקַטַּלְנוּ
יְקַטֵּל	יְקֻטַּל	יַקְטִיל	יָקְטַל	יִתְקַטֵּל
תְּקַטֵּל	תְּקֻטַּל	תַּקְטִיל	תָּקְטַל	תִּתְקַטֵּל
תְּקַטֵּל	תְּקֻטַּל	תַּקְטִיל	תָּקְטַל	תִּתְקַטֵּל
תְּקַטְּלִי	תְּקֻטְּלִי	תַּקְטִילִי	תָּקְטְלִי	תִּתְקַטְּלִי
אֲקַטֵּל	אֲקֻטַּל	אַקְטִיל	אָקְטַל	אֶתְקַטֵּל
יְקַטְּלוּ	יְקֻטְּלוּ	יַקְטִילוּ	יָקְטְלוּ	יִתְקַטְּלוּ
תְּקַטֵּלְנָה	תְּקֻטַּלְנָה	תַּקְטֵלְנָה	תָּקְטַלְנָה	תִּתְקַטֵּלְנָה
תְּקַטְּלוּ	תְּקֻטְּלוּ	תַּקְטִילוּ	תָּקְטְלוּ	תִּתְקַטְּלוּ
תְּקַטֵּלְנָה	תְּקֻטַּלְנָה	תַּקְטֵלְנָה	תָּקְטַלְנָה	תִּתְקַטֵּלְנָה
נְקַטֵּל	נְקֻטַּל	נַקְטִיל	נָקְטַל	נִתְקַטֵּל

2. or קֻטַּל   1. or הִתְקַטֵּל

The Regular Verb

	Qal. Active	Qal Stative		Niph'al
Cohort. 1 sg.	אֶקְטְלָה	אֶכְבְּדָה		אֶקָטְלָה
Juss. 3 sg. m.	יִקְטֹל	יִכְבַּד		יִקָטֵל
Waw cons. impft.	וַיִּקְטֹל	וַיִּכְבַּד		וַיִּקָטֵל
waw cons. pft.	וְקָטַלְתָּ	וְכָבַדְתָּ		וְתֶקָטַלְתָּ
Imperative Sing. 2 m.	¹קְטֹל	כְּבַד		הִקָּטֵל
2 f.	קִטְלִי	כִּבְדִי		הִקָּטְלִי
Plur. 2 m.	קִטְלוּ	כִּבְדוּ		הִקָּטְלוּ
2 f.	קְטֹלְנָה	כְּבַדְנָה		הִקָּטַלְנָה
Infinitive constr.	קְטֹל	כְּבַד		הִקָּטֵל
absol.	קָטוֹל	כָּבוֹד		הִקָּטֹל, נִקְטֹל
Participle active	קֹטֵל	כָּבֵד	קָטֹן	
passive	קָטוּל			נִקְטָל

1. קְטְלָה (emphatic imperative).

The Regular Verb

Pi'el	Pu'al	Hiph'il	Hoph'al	Hithpa'el
אֲקַטְּלָה		אַקְטִילָה		אֶתְקַטְּלָה
יְקַטֵּל	יְקֻטַּל	יַקְטֵל	יֻקְטַל	יִתְקַטֵּל
וַיְקַטֵּל	וַיְקֻטַּל	וַיַּקְטֵל	וַיֻּקְטַל	וַיִּתְקַטֵּל
וְקִטַּלְתָּ		וְהִקְטַלְתָּ		
קַטֵּל		הַקְטֵל		הִתְקַטֵּל
קַטְּלִי		הַקְטִילִי		הִתְקַטְּלִי
קַטְּלוּ		הַקְטִילוּ		הִתְקַטְּלוּ
קַטֵּלְנָה		הַקְטֵלְנָה		הִתְקַטֵּלְנָה
קַטֵּל		הַקְטִיל	(הָקְטַל)	הִתְקַטֵּל
קַטֹּל, קַטֵּל	קֻטַּל	הַקְטֵל	(הָקְטֵל)	הִתְקַטֵּל
מְקַטֵּל		מַקְטִיל	מָקְטָל	מִתְקַטֵּל
	מְקֻטָּל			

The Regular Verb with Suffixes
Perfect Qal

	3 sg. m. קָטַל	3 sg. f. קָטְלָה	2 sg. m. קָטַלְתָּ	2 sg. f. קָטַלְתְּ
Suffixes				
sing. 1 c.	קְטָלַנִי	קְטָלַתְנִי	קְטַלְתַּנִי	קְטַלְתִּינִי
2 m.	קְטָלְךָ	קְטָלַתְךָ		
2 f.	קְטָלֵךְ	קְטָלָתֶךְ		
3 m.	קְטָלוֹ	קְטָלַתְהוּ	קְטַלְתָּהוּ	קְטַלְתִּיהוּ
	קְטָלָהוּ	קְטָלַתּוּ	קְטַלְתּוֹ	
3 f.	קְטָלָהּ	קְטָלָתָּה	קְטַלְתָּהּ	קְטַלְתִּיהָ
plur. 1 c.	קְטָלָנוּ	קְטָלַתְנוּ	קְטַלְתָּנוּ	קְטַלְתִּינוּ
2 m.	קְטַלְכֶם			
2 f.	קְטַלְכֶן			
3 m.	קְטָלָם	קְטָלָתַם	קְטַלְתָּם	קְטַלְתִּים
3 f.	קְטָלָן	קְטָלָתַן	קְטַלְתָּן	קְטַלְתִּין

THE REGULAR VERB WITH SUFFIXES
PERFECT QAL

	1 sg. c. קָטַלְתִּי	3 pl. c. קָטְלוּ	2 pl. m. קְטַלְתֶּם	1 pl. c. קָטַלְנוּ
Suffixes				
sing. 1 c.		קְטָלוּנִי	קְטַלְתּוּנִי	
2 m.	קְטַלְתִּיךָ	קְטָלוּךָ		קְטַלְנוּךָ
2 f.	קְטַלְתִּיךְ	קְטָלוּךְ		קְטַלְנוּךְ
3 m.	קְטַלְתִּיהוּ	קְטָלוּהוּ	קְטַלְתּוּהוּ	קְטַלְנוּהוּ
	קְטַלְתִּיו		etc.	etc.
3 f.	קְטַלְתִּיהָ	קְטָלוּהָ		
plur. 1 c.		קְטָלוּנוּ		
2 m.	קְטַלְתִּיכֶם			
2 f.	קְטַלְתִּיכֶן			
3 m.	קְטַלְתִּים	קְטָלוּם		
3 f.	קְטַלְתִּין	קְטָלוּן		

The Regular Verb with Suffixes

	Imperfect Qal		Imperative		Infin. Constr.
	3 sg. m.	3 pl. m.	sing.	plur.	
	יִקְטֹל	יִקְטְלוּ	קְטֹל	קִטְלוּ	קְטֹל
Suffixes					
sg. 1 c.	יִקְטְלֵנִי	יִקְטְלוּנִי	קְטְלֵנִי	קִטְלוּנִי	קָטְלִי, קְטָלֵנִי
2 m.	יִקְטָלְךָ	יִקְטְלוּךָ			קָטְלְךָ, קְטָלְךָ
2 f.	יִקְטְלֵךְ	יִקְטְלוּךְ			קָטְלֵךְ
3 m.	יִקְטְלֵהוּ	יִקְטְלוּהוּ	קְטְלֵהוּ	קִטְלוּהוּ	קָטְלוֹ
3 f.	יִקְטְלֶהָ	יִקְטְלוּהָ	קְטְלֶהָ	etc.	קָטְלָהּ
pl. 1 c.	יִקְטְלֵנוּ	יִקְטְלוּנוּ	קְטְלֵנוּ		קָטְלֵנוּ
2 m.	יִקְטָלְכֶם	יִקְטְלוּכֶם			קָטְלְכֶם, קְטָלְכֶם
2 f.	יִקְטָלְכֶן	יִקְטְלוּכֶן			קָטְלְכֶן, קְטָלְכֶן
3 m.	יִקְטְלֵם	יִקְטְלוּם	קְטְלֵם		קָטְלָם
3 f.	יִקְטְלֵן	יִקְטְלוּן	קְטְלֵן		קָטְלָן

THE REGULAR VERB WITH SUFFIXES

	Pi'el		Hiph'il	
	Perfect 3 sg. m. קִטֵּל	Imperfect 3 sg. m. יְקַטֵּל	Perfect 3 sg. m. הִקְטִיל	Imperfect 3 sg. m. יַקְטִיל
Suffixes				
sg. 1 c.	קִטְּלַנִי	יְקַטְּלֵנִי	הִקְטִילַנִי	יַקְטִילֵנִי
2 m.	קִטֶּלְךָ	יְקַטֶּלְךָ	הִקְטִילְךָ	יַקְטִילְךָ
2 f.	קִטְּלֵךְ	יְקַטְּלֵךְ	הִקְטִילֵךְ	יַקְטִילֵךְ
3 m.	קִטְּלוֹ	יְקַטְּלֵהוּ	etc.	etc.
3 f.	קִטְּלָהּ	יְקַטְּלֶהָ		
pl. 1 c.	קִטְּלָנוּ	יְקַטְּלֵנוּ		
	etc.	etc.		

PE NUN VERB

	Qal		Niph'al	Hiph'il
Perfect				
Sing. 3 m.	נָפַל	(נָגַשׁ)	נִגַּשׁ	הִגִּישׁ
3 f.		regular	נִגְּשָׁה	הִגִּישָׁה
2 m.			נִגַּשְׁתָּ	הִגַּשְׁתָּ
2 f.			נִגַּשְׁתְּ	הִגַּשְׁתְּ
1 c.			נִגַּשְׁתִּי	הִגַּשְׁתִּי
Plur. 3 c.			נִגְּשׁוּ	הִגִּישׁוּ
2 m.			נִגַּשְׁתֶּם	הִגַּשְׁתֶּם
2 f.			נִגַּשְׁתֶּן	הִגַּשְׁתֶּן
1 c.			נִגַּשְׁנוּ	הִגַּשְׁנוּ
Imperfect				
Sing. 3 m.	יִפֹּל	יִגַּשׁ	יִנָּגֵשׁ	יַגִּישׁ
3 f.	תִּפֹּל	תִּגַּשׁ	etc.	תַּגִּישׁ
2 m.	תִּפֹּל	תִּגַּשׁ		תַּגִּישׁ
2 f.	תִּפְּלִי	תִּגְּשִׁי		תַּגִּישִׁי
1 c.	אֶפֹּל	אֶגַּשׁ		אַגִּישׁ
Plur. 3 m.	יִפְּלוּ	יִגְּשׁוּ		יַגִּישׁוּ
3 f.	תִּפֹּלְנָה	תִּגַּשְׁנָה		תַּגֵּשְׁנָה
2 m.	תִּפְּלוּ	תִּגְּשׁוּ		תַּגִּישׁוּ
2 f.	תִּפֹּלְנָה	תִּגַּשְׁנָה		תַּגֵּשְׁנָה
1 c.	נִפֹּל	נִגַּשׁ		נַגִּישׁ

PE NUN VERB

		Hoph'al	Qal		Niph'al	
Perfect						
Sing.	3 m.	הֻגַּשׁ	נָתַן	לָקַח	נִלְקַח	נִתַּן
	3 f.	הֻגְּשָׁה	נָתְנָה		נִתְּנָה	
	2 m.	הֻגַּשְׁתָּ	נָתַתָּ		נִתַּתָּ	
	2 f.		נָתַתְּ	regular	regular	
	1 c.	etc.	נָתַתִּי			
Plur.	3 c.		נָתְנוּ			
	2 m.		נְתַתֶּם			
	2 f.		נְתַתֶּן			
	1 c.		נָתַנּוּ			
Imperfect						
Sing.	3 m.	יֻגַּשׁ	יִתֵּן	יִקַּח	יִלָּקַח	יִנָּתֵן
	3 f.	תֻּגַּשׁ	תִּתֵּן	תִּקַּח		
	2 m.	תֻּגַּשׁ	תִּתֵּן	תִּקַּח		
	2 f.	etc.	תִּתְּנִי	תִּקְּחִי	etc.	
	1 c.		אֶתֵּן	אֶקַּח		
Plur.	3 m.		יִתְּנוּ	יִקְּחוּ		
	3 f.		(תִּתֵּנָּה)	תִּקַּחְנָה		
	2 m.		תִּתְּנוּ	תִּקְּחוּ		
	2 f.		(תִּתֵּנָּה)	תִּקַּחְנָה		
	1 c.		נִתֵּן	נִקַּח		

Pᴇ Nᴜɴ Vᴇʀʙ

	Qal		Niph'al	Hiph'il
Cohor. 1 sg.	אֶגְּשָׁה	אֶפְּלָה		אַגִּשָׁה
Juss. 3 sg. m.	יִגַּשׁ	יִפֹּל		יַגֵּשׁ
Waw cons. imp.	וַיִּגַּשׁ	וַיִּפֹּל		וַיַּגֵּשׁ
Waw cons. pft.		וְנָפַלְתָּ		
Imperative				
Sing. 2 m.	גַּשׁ (שֶׁת)	נְפֹל	הִנָּגֵשׁ	הַגֵּשׁ
2 f.	גְּשִׁי	נִפְלִי	הִנָּגְשִׁי	הַגִּישִׁי
Plur. 2 m.	גְּשׁוּ	נִפְלוּ	הִנָּגְשׁוּ	הַגִּישׁוּ
2 f.	גַּשְׁנָה	נְפֹלְנָה	הִנָּגַשְׁנָה	הַגֵּשְׁנָה
Infinitive constr.	גֶּשֶׁת	נְפֹל	הִנָּגֵשׁ	הַגִּישׁ
absol.	נָגוֹשׁ	נָפוֹל	הִנָּגֵשׁ	הַגֵּשׁ
Participle active	(נֹגֵשׁ)	נֹפֵל	נִגָּשׁ	מַגִּישׁ
passive	(נָגוּשׁ)			

Pᴇ Nᴜɴ Vᴇʀʙ

	Hophʻal	Qal		Niphʻal
Cohor. 1 sg.		אֶתְּנָה	אֶקְחָה	
Juss. 3 sg. m.	יֻגַּשׁ	יִתֵּן	יִקַּח	
Waw cons. imp.	וַיֻּגַּשׁ	וַיִּתֵּן	וַיִּקַּח	
Waw cons. pft.		וְנָתַתָּ		
Imperative				
Sing. 2 m.		תֵּן, תְּנָה	קַח, קְחָה	הִלָּקַח הִנָּתֵן
2 m.		תְּנִי	קְחִי	etc.
Plur. 2 m.		תְּנוּ	קְחוּ	
2 f.		(תֵּנָּה)	(קְחֶנָה)	
Infinitive constr.	הֻגַּשׁ	¹תֵּת	²קַחַת	הִלָּקַח הִנָּתֵן
absol.	הֻגֵּשׁ	נָתוֹן	לָקוֹחַ	הִלָּקֹחַ הִנָּתֹן
Participle active		נֹתֵן	לֹקֵחַ	
passive	מֻגָּשׁ	נָתוּן	לָקוּחַ	נִלְקָח נִתָּן

1. with suffixes תִּתִּי etc.   2. with suffixes קַחְתִּי etc.

PE GUTTURAL VERBS

		Qal		Niph'al	Hiph'il
		Active	Stative		
Perfect					
Sing.	3 m.	עָמַד	חָזַק	נֶעֱמַד	הֶעֱמִיד
	3 f.	עָמְדָה	etc.	נֶעֶמְדָה	הֶעֱמִידָה
	2 m.	עָמַדְתָּ		נֶעֱמַדְתָּ	הֶעֱמַדְתָּ
	2 f.	עָמַדְתְּ		נֶעֱמַדְתְּ	הֶעֱמַדְתְּ
	1 c.	עָמַדְתִּי		נֶעֱמַדְתִּי	הֶעֱמַדְתִּי
Plur.	3 c.	עָמְדוּ		נֶעֶמְדוּ	הֶעֱמִידוּ
	2 m.	עֲמַדְתֶּם		נֶעֱמַדְתֶּם	הֶעֱמַדְתֶּם
	2 f.	עֲמַדְתֶּן		נֶעֱמַדְתֶּן	הֶעֱמַדְתֶּן
	1 c.	עָמַדְנוּ		נֶעֱמַדְנוּ	הֶעֱמַדְנוּ
Imperfect					
Sing.	3 m.	יַעֲמֹד	יֶחֱזַק	יֵעָמֵד	יַעֲמִיד
	3 f.	תַּעֲמֹד	תֶּחֱזַק	תֵּעָמֵד	תַּעֲמִיד
	2 m.	תַּעֲמֹד	תֶּחֱזַק	תֵּעָמֵד	תַּעֲמִיד
	2 f.	תַּעַמְדִי	תֶּחֶזְקִי	תֵּעָמְדִי	תַּעֲמִידִי
	1 c.	אֶעֱמֹד	אֶחֱזַק	אֵעָמֵד	אַעֲמִיד
Plur.	3 m.	יַעַמְדוּ	יֶחֶזְקוּ	יֵעָמְדוּ	יַעֲמִידוּ
	3 f.	תַּעֲמֹדְנָה	תֶּחֱזַקְנָה	תֵּעָמַדְנָה	תַּעֲמֵדְנָה
	2 m.	תַּעַמְדוּ	תֶּחֶזְקוּ	תֵּעָמְדוּ	תַּעֲמִידוּ
	2 f.	תַּעֲמֹדְנָה	תֶּחֱזַקְנָה	תֵּעָמַדְנָה	תַּעֲמֵדְנָה
	1 c.	נַעֲמֹד	נֶחֱזַק	נֵעָמֵד	נַעֲמִיד

Pe Guttural Verbs

		Hoph'al	Qal
Perfect			
Sing.	3 m.	הָעֳמַד	אָכַל
	3 f.	הָעֳמְדָה	regular
	2 m.	הָעֳמַדְתָּ	
	2 f.	הָעֳמַדְתְּ	
	1 c.	הָעֳמַדְתִּי	
Plur.	3 c.	הָעֳמְדוּ	
	2 m.	הָעֳמַדְתֶּם	
	2 f.	הָעֳמַדְתֶּן	
	1 c.	הָעֳמַדְנוּ	
Imperfect			
Sing.	3 m.	יָעֳמַד	יֹאכַל
	3 f.	תָּעֳמַד	תֹּאכַל
	2 m.	תָּעֳמַד	תֹּאכַל
	2 f.	תָּעֳמְדִי	תֹּאכְלִי
	1 c.	אָעֳמַד	אֹכַל
Plur.	3 m.	יָעֳמְדוּ	יֹאכְלוּ
	3 f.	תָּעֳמַדְנָה	תֹּאכַלְנָה
	2 m.	תָּעֳמְדוּ	תֹּאכְלוּ
	2 f.	תָּעֳמַדְנָה	תֹּאכַלְנָה
	1 c.	נָעֳמַד	נֹאכַל

Pɛ Guttural Verbs

	Qal		Niph'al	Hiph'il
Cohor. 1 sg.	אֶעֶמְדָה			אַעֲמִידָה
Juss. 3 sg. m.	יַעֲמֹד	יֶחֱזַק		יַעֲמֵד
Waw cons. imp.	וַיַּעֲמֹד	וַיֶּחֱזַק		וַיַּעֲמֵד
Waw cons. pft.	וְעָמַדְתָּ			וְהַעֲמַדְתָּ
Imperative				
Sing. 2 m.	עֲמֹד	חֲזַק	הֵעָמֵד	הַעֲמֵד
2 f.	עִמְדִי	חִזְקִי	הֵעָמְדִי	הַעֲמִידִי
Plur. 2 m.	עִמְדוּ	חִזְקוּ	הֵעָמְדוּ	הַעֲמִידוּ
2 f.	עֲמֹדְנָה	חֲזַקְנָה	הֵעָמַדְנָה	הַעֲמֵדְנָה
Infinitive constr.	עֲמֹד		הֵעָמֵד	הַעֲמִיד
absol.	עָמוֹד		נַעֲמֹד	הַעֲמֵד
Participle active	עֹמֵד		נֶעֱמָד	מַעֲמִיד
passive	עָמוּד			

Pe Guttural Verbs

	Hoph'al	Qal
Cohor. 1 sg.		אֹכְלָה
Juss. 3 sg. m.		יֹאכַל
Waw cons. impft.		וַיֹּאכַל
Waw cons. pft.		וְאָכַלְתָּ
Imperative Sing. 2 m.		אֱכֹל
2 f.		אִכְלִי
Plur. 2 m.		אִכְלוּ
2 f.		אֲכֹלְנָה
Infinitive constr.		אֱכֹל
absol.	הָעֲמֵד	אָכוֹל
Participle active		אֹכֵל
passive	מָעֳמָד	אָכוּל

'AYIN GUTTURAL VERBS

		Qal	Niph'al	Pi'el	Pu'al	Hithpa'el
Perfect						
sing.	3 m.	בָּחַר	נִבְחַר	בֵּרַךְ	בֹּרַךְ	הִתְבָּרַךְ
	3 f.	בָּחֲרָה	נִבְחֲרָה	בֵּרֲכָה	בֹּרְכָה	הִתְבָּרְכָה
	2 m.	בָּחַרְתָּ	נִבְחַרְתָּ	בֵּרַכְתָּ	בֹּרַכְתָּ	הִתְבָּרַכְתָּ
	2 f.	בָּחַרְתְּ	etc.	בֵּרַכְתְּ	etc.	הִתְבָּרַכְתְּ
	1 c.	בָּחַרְתִּי		בֵּרַכְתִּי		הִתְבָּרַכְתִּי
plur.	3 c.	בָּחֲרוּ		בֵּרֲכוּ		הִתְבָּרֲכוּ
	2 m.	בְּחַרְתֶּם		בֵּרַכְתֶּם		הִתְבָּרַכְתֶּם
	2 f.	בְּחַרְתֶּן		בֵּרַכְתֶּן		הִתְבָּרַכְתֶּן
	1 c.	בָּחַרְנוּ		בֵּרַכְנוּ		הִתְבָּרַכְנוּ
Imperfect						
sing.	3 m.	יִבְחַר	יִבָּחֵר	יְבָרֵךְ	יְבֹרַךְ	יִתְבָּרַךְ
	3 f.	תִּבְחַר	תִּבָּחֵר	תְּבָרֵךְ	תְּבֹרַךְ	תִּתְבָּרַךְ
	2 m.	תִּבְחַר	תִּבָּחֵר	תְּבָרֵךְ	תְּבֹרַךְ	תִּתְבָּרַךְ
	2 f.	תִּבְחֲרִי	תִּבָּחֲרִי	תְּבָרֲכִי	תְּבֹרְכִי	תִּתְבָּרֲכִי
	1 c.	אֶבְחַר	אֶבָּחֵר	אֲבָרֵךְ	אֲבֹרַךְ	אֶתְבָּרַךְ
plur.	3 m.	יִבְחֲרוּ	יִבָּחֲרוּ	יְבָרֲכוּ	יְבֹרְכוּ	יִתְבָּרֲכוּ
	3 f.	תִּבְחַרְנָה	תִּבָּחַרְנָה	תְּבָרֵכְנָה	תְּבֹרַכְנָה	תִּתְבָּרֵכְנָה
	2 m.	תִּבְחֲרוּ	תִּבָּחֲרוּ	תְּבָרֲכוּ	תְּבֹרְכוּ	תִּתְבָּרֲכוּ
	2 f.	תִּבְחַרְנָה	תִּבָּחַרְנָה	תְּבָרֵכְנָה	תְּבֹרַכְנָה	תִּתְבָּרֵכְנָה
	1 c.	נִבְחַר	נִבָּחֵר	נְבָרֵךְ	נְבֹרַךְ	נִתְבָּרֵךְ

'Ayin Guttural Verbs

	Qal	Niph'al	Pi'el	Pu'al	Hithpa'el
Cohor. 1 sg.	אֶבְחֲרָה	אִבָּחֲרָה	אֲבָרְכָה		
Juss. 3 sg. m.	יִבְחַר	יִבָּחֵר	יְבָרֵךְ		
Waw cons. imp.	וַיִּבְחַר	וַיִּבָּחֵר	וַיְבָרֶךְ		
Waw cons. pf.	וּבָחַרְתָּ	וְנִבְחַרְתָּ			
Imperative					
sing. 2 m.	בְּחַר	הִבָּחֵר	בָּרֵךְ		הִתְבָּרֵךְ
2 f.	בַּחֲרִי	הִבָּחֲרִי	בָּרְכִי		הִתְבָּרְכִי
plur. 2 m.	בַּחֲרוּ	הִבָּחֲרוּ	בָּרְכוּ		הִתְבָּרְכוּ
2 f.	בְּחַרְנָה	הִבָּחַרְנָה	בָּרֵכְנָה		הִתְבָּרֵכְנָה
Infinitive					
constr..	בְּחֹר	הִבָּחֵר	בָּרֵךְ	בֹּרַךְ	הִתְבָּרֵךְ
absol.	בָּחוֹר	נִבְחֹר	בָּרֵךְ		
Participle					
active	בֹּחֵר		מְבָרֵךְ		מִתְבָּרֵךְ
passive	בָּחוּר	נִבְחָר		מְבֹרָךְ	

LAMEDH GUTTURAL VERBS

		Qal	Niph'al	Pi'el
Perfect				
sing.	3 m.	שָׁלַח	נִשְׁלַח	שִׁלַּח
	3 f.	שָׁלְחָה	נִשְׁלְחָה	שִׁלְּחָה
	2 m.	שָׁלַחְתָּ	נִשְׁלַחְתָּ	שִׁלַּחְתָּ
	2 f.	שָׁלַחַתְּ	etc.	etc.
	1 c.	שָׁלַחְתִּי		
plur.	3 c.	שָׁלְחוּ		
	2 m.	שְׁלַחְתֶּם		
	2 f.	שְׁלַחְתֶּן		
	1 c.	שָׁלַחְנוּ		
Imperfect				
sing.	3m.	יִשְׁלַח	יִשָּׁלַח	יְשַׁלַּח
	3 f.	תִּשְׁלַח	תִּשָּׁלַח	תְּשַׁלַּח
	2 m.	תִּשְׁלַח	תִּשָּׁלַח	תְּשַׁלַּח
	2 f.	תִּשְׁלְחִי	תִּשָּׁלְחִי	תְּשַׁלְּחִי
	1 c.	אֶשְׁלַח	אֶשָּׁלַח	אֲשַׁלַּח
plur.	3 m.	יִשְׁלְחוּ	יִשָּׁלְחוּ	יְשַׁלְּחוּ
	3 f.	תִּשְׁלַחְנָה	תִּשָּׁלַחְנָה	תְּשַׁלַּחְנָה
	2 m.	תִּשְׁלְחוּ	תִּשָּׁלְחוּ	תְּשַׁלְּחוּ
	2 f.	תִּשְׁלַחְנָה	תִּשָּׁלַחְנָה	תְּשַׁלַּחְנָה
	1 c.	נִשְׁלַח	נִשָּׁלַח	נְשַׁלַּח

LAMEDH GUTTURAL VERBS

		Pu'al	Hiph'il	Hoph'al	Hithpa'el
Perfect					
sing.	3 m.	שֻׁלַּח	הִשְׁלִיחַ	הָשְׁלַח	הִשְׁתַּלַּח
	3 f.	שֻׁלְּחָה	הִשְׁלִיחָה	הָשְׁלְחָה	הִשְׁתַּלְּחָה
	2 m.	שֻׁלַּחְתָּ	הִשְׁלַחְתָּ	הָשְׁלַחְתָּ	הִשְׁתַּלַּחְתָּ
	2 f.	etc.	הִשְׁלַחַתְּ	etc.	etc.
	1 c.		הִשְׁלַחְתִּי		
plur.	3 c.		הִשְׁלִיחוּ		
	2 m.		הִשְׁלַחְתֶּם		
	2 f.		הִשְׁלַחְתֶּן		
	1 c.		הִשְׁלַחְנוּ		
Imperfect					
sing.	3 m.	יְשֻׁלַּח	יַשְׁלִיחַ	יָשְׁלַח	יִשְׁתַּלַּח
	3 f.	תְּשֻׁלַּח	תַּשְׁלִיחַ	תָּשְׁלַח	תִּשְׁתַּלַּח
	2 m.	תְּשֻׁלַּח	תַּשְׁלִיחַ	תָּשְׁלַח	תִּשְׁתַּלַּח
	2 f.	etc.	תַּשְׁלִיחִי	etc.	etc.
	1 c.		אַשְׁלִיחַ		
plur.	3 m.		יַשְׁלִיחוּ		
	3 f.		תַּשְׁלַחְנָה		
	2 m.		תַּשְׁלִיחוּ		
	2 f.		תַּשְׁלַחְנָה		
	1 c.		נַשְׁלִיחַ		

LAMEDH GUTTURAL VERBS

		Qal	Niph'al	Pi'el
Cohor. 1 sg.		אֶשְׁלְחָה	אִשָּׁלְחָה	אֲשַׁלְּחָה
Juss. 3 sg. m.		יִשְׁלַח	יִשָּׁלַח	יְשַׁלַּח
Waw cons. imp.		וַיִּשְׁלַח	וַיִּשָּׁלַח	וַיְשַׁלַּח
Waw cons. pf.		וְשָׁלַחְתָּ		
Imperative				
sing.	2 m.	שְׁלַח	הִשָּׁלַח	שַׁלַּח
	2 f.	שִׁלְחִי	הִשָּׁלְחִי	שַׁלְּחִי
plur.	2 m.	שִׁלְחוּ	הִשָּׁלְחוּ	שַׁלְּחוּ
	2 f.	שְׁלַחְנָה	הִשָּׁלַחְנָה	שַׁלַּחְנָה
Infinitive constr.		שְׁלֹחַ	הִשָּׁלַח	שַׁלַּח
	absol.	שָׁלֹחַ	נִשְׁלֹחַ	שַׁלֵּחַ
Participle active		שֹׁלֵחַ		מְשַׁלֵּחַ
	passive	שָׁלוּחַ	נִשְׁלָח	

LAMEDH GUTTURAL VERBS

	Pu'al	Hiph'il	Hoph'al	Hithpa'el
Cohor. 1 sg.		אֶשְׁלִיחָה		
Juss. 3 sg. m.		יַשְׁלַח		
Waw cons. imp		וַיַּשְׁלַח		
Waw cons. pf.				
Imperative				הִשְׁתַּלַּח
sing. 2 m.		הַשְׁלַח		
2 ff.		הַשְׁלִיחִי		הִשְׁתַּלְּחִי
plural 2 m.		הַשְׁלִיחוּ		הִשְׁתַּלְּחוּ
2 f.		הַשְׁלַחְנָה		הִשְׁתַּלַּחְנָה
Infinitive				
constr.		הַשְׁלִיחַ		הִשְׁתַּלַּח
absol.		הַשְׁלֵחַ	הָשְׁלַח	
Participle				
active		מַשְׁלִיחַ		מִשְׁתַּלַּח
passive	מְשֻׁלָּח		מֻשְׁלָח	

LAMEDH 'ALEPH VERBS
Qal

		Active	Stative	Niph'al	Pi'el
Perfect					
sing.	3 m.	מָצָא	מָלֵא	נִמְצָא	מִצֵּא
	3 f.	מָצְאָה	מָלְאָה	נִמְצְאָה	מִצְּאָה
	2 m.	מָצָאתָ	מָלֵאתָ	נִמְצֵאתָ	מִצֵּאתָ
	2 f.	מָצָאת	מָלֵאת	נִמְצֵאת	etc.
	1 c.	מָצָאתִי	מָלֵאתִי	נִמְצֵאתִי	as
					Niph.
plur.	3 c.	מָצְאוּ	מָלְאוּ	נִמְצְאוּ	
	2 m.	מְצָאתֶם	מְלֵאתֶם	נִמְצֵאתֶם	
	2 f.	מְצָאתֶן	מְלֵאתֶן	נִמְצֵאתֶן	
	1 c.	מָצָאנוּ	מָלֵאנוּ	נִמְצֵאנוּ	
Imperfect					
sing.	3 m.	יִמְצָא	יִמְלָא	יִמָּצֵא	יְמַצֵּא
	3 f.	תִּמְצָא	etc.	תִּמָּצֵא	תְּמַצֵּא
	2 m.	תִּמְצָא		תִּמָּצֵא	תְּמַצֵּא
	2 f.	תִּמְצְאִי		תִּמָּצְאִי	תְּמַצְּאִי
	1 c.	אֶמְצָא		אֶמָּצֵא	אֲמַצֵּא
plur.	3 m.	יִמְצְאוּ		יִמָּצְאוּ	etc.
	3 f.	תִּמְצֶאנָה		תִּמָּצֶאנָה	as
	2 m.	תִּמְצְאוּ		תִּמָּצְאוּ	Niph.
	2 f.	תִּמְצֶאנָה		תִּמָּצֶאנָה	
	1 c.	נִמְצָא		נִמָּצֵא	

LAMEDH 'ALEPH VERBS

	Pu'al	Hiph'il	Hoph'al	Hithpa'el
Perfect				
sing. 3 m.	מֻצָּא	הִמְצִיא	הֻמְצָא	הִתְמַצָּא
3 f.	מֻצְּאָה	הִמְצִיאָה	הֻמְצְאָה	הִתְמַצְּאָה
3 m.	מֻצֵּאתָ	הִמְצֵאתָ	הֻמְצֵאתָ	הִתְמַצֵּאתָ
2 f.	etc.	הִמְצֵאת	etc.	etc.
1 c.	as	הִמְצֵאתִי	as	as
	Niph.		Niph.	Niph.
plur. 3 c.		הִמְצִיאוּ		
2 m.		הִמְצֵאתֶם		
2 f.		הִמְצֵאתֶן		
1 c.		הִמְצֵאנוּ		
Imperfect				
sing. 3 m.	יְמֻצָּא	יַמְצִיא	יֻמְצָא	יִתְמַצָּא
3 f.	תְּמֻצָּא	תַּמְצִיא	תֻּמְצָא	תִּתְמַצָּא
2 m.	תְּמֻצָּא	תַּמְצִיא	תֻּמְצָא	תִּתְמַצָּא
2 f.	etc.	תַּמְצִיאִי	etc.	etc.
1 c.	as	אַמְצִיא	as	as
plur. 3 m.	Qal	יַמְצִיאוּ	Qal	Niph.
3 f.		תַּמְצֶאנָה		
2 m.		תַּמְצִיאוּ		
2 f.		תַּמְצֶאנָה		
1 c.		נַמְצִיא		

LAMEDH 'ALEPH VERBS

Qal

	Active	Stative	Niph'al	Pi'el
Cohor. 1 sg.	אֶמְצְאָה		אִמָּצְאָה	
Juss. 3 sg. m.	יִמְצָא		יִמָּצֵא	
Waw cons. imp.	וַיִּמְצָא		וַיִּמָּצֵא	
Waw cons. pf.	וּמָצָאתָ			
Imperative				
sing. 2 m.	מְצָא		הִמָּצֵא	מַצֵּא
2 f.	מִצְאִי		הִמָּצְאִי	etc.
				as
plur. 2 m.	מִצְאוּ		הִמָּצְאוּ	Niph.
2 f.	מְצֶאנָה		הִמָּצֶאנָה	
Infinitive				
constr.	מְצֹא		הִמָּצֵא	מַצֵּא
absol.	מָצוֹא		נִמְצֹא	מַצֹּא
Participle				
active	מֹצֵא			מְמַצֵּא
passive	מָצוּא		נִמְצָא	

LAMEDH 'ALEPH VERBS

	Pu'al	Hiph'il	Hoph'al	Hithpa'el
Cohor. 1 sg.		אַמְצִיאָה		
Juss. 3 sg. m.		יַמְצֵא		
Waw cons imp.		וַיַּמְצֵא		
Waw cons. pf.				
Imperative				
sing. 2 m.		הַמְצֵא		הִתְמַצֵּא
2 f.		הַמְצִיאִי		הִתְמַצְּאִי
				etc.
plur. 2 m.		הַמְצִיאוּ		as
				Niph.
2 f.		הַמְצֶאנָה		
Infinitive				
constr.		הַמְצִיא	הֻמְצָא	הִתְמַצֵּא
absol.		הַמְצֵא		
Participle				
active		מַמְצִיא		מִתְמַצֵּא
passive	מְמֻצָּא		מֻמְצָא	

PE WAW AND PE YODH VERBS

		Qal		Niph'al	Hiph'il	Hoph'al
Perfect						
sing.	3 m.	יָרֵא	יָשַׁב	נוֹשַׁב	הוֹשִׁיב	הוּשַׁב
	3 f.		יָשְׁבָה	נוֹשְׁבָה	הוֹשִׁיבָה	הוּשְׁבָה
	2 m.		יָשַׁבְתָּ	נוֹשַׁבְתָּ	הוֹשַׁבְתָּ	הוּשַׁבְתָּ
	2 f.	etc.		etc.	etc.	etc.
	1 c.					
plur.	3 c.					
	2 m.					
	2 f.					
	1 c.					
Imperfect						
sing.	3 m.	יִירָא	יֵשֵׁב	יִוָּשֵׁב	יוֹשִׁיב	יוּשַׁב
	3 f.		תֵּשֵׁב	תִּוָּשֵׁב	תּוֹשִׁיב	תּוּשַׁב
	2 m.		תֵּשֵׁב	תִּוָּשֵׁב	תּוֹשִׁיב	תּוּשַׁב
	2 f.		תֵּשְׁבִי	תִּוָּשְׁבִי	תּוֹשִׁיבִי	etc.
	1 c.		אֵשֵׁב	אִוָּשֵׁב	אוֹשִׁיב	
plur.	3 m.		יֵשְׁבוּ	יִוָּשְׁבוּ	יוֹשִׁיבוּ	
	3 f.		תֵּשַׁבְנָה	תִּוָּשַׁבְנָה	(תּוֹשַׁבְנָה)	
	2 m.		תֵּשְׁבוּ	תִּוָּשְׁבוּ	תּוֹשִׁיבוּ	
	2 f.		תֵּשַׁבְנָה	תִּוָּשַׁבְנָה	(תּוֹשַׁבְנָה)	
	1 c.		נֵשֵׁב	נִוָּשֵׁב	נוֹשִׁיב	

PE WAW AND PE YODH VERBS

		Qal.	Hiph'il
Perfect			
sing.	3 m.	יָשַׁב	הֵישִׁיב
	3 f.	יָשְׁבָה	הֵישִׁיבָה
	2 m.	etc.	הֵישַׁבְתָּ
	2 f.		הֵישַׁבְתְּ
	1 c.		הֵישַׁבְתִּי
plur.	3 c.		הֵישִׁיבוּ
	2 m.		הֵישַׁבְתֶּם
	2 f.		הֵישַׁבְתֶּן
	1 c.		הֵישַׁבְנוּ
Imperfect			
sing.	3 m.	יֵישֵׁב	יֵישִׁיב
	3 f.	תֵּישֵׁב	תֵּישִׁיב
	2 m.	תֵּישֵׁב	תֵּישִׁיב
	2 f.	תֵּישְׁבִי	תֵּישִׁיבִי
	1 c.	אֵישֵׁב	אֵישִׁיב
plur.	3 m.	יֵישְׁבוּ	יֵישִׁיבוּ
	3 f.	תֵּישַׁבְנָה	תֵּישֵׁבְנָה
	2 m.	תֵּישְׁבוּ	תֵּישִׁיבוּ
	2 f.	תֵּישַׁבְנָה	תֵּישֵׁבְנָה
	1 c.	נֵישֵׁב	נֵישִׁיב

Pe Waw and Pe Yodh Verbs

	Qal	Niph'al	Hiph'il	Hoph'al
Cohor. 1 sg.	אֶשְׁבָה			
Juss. 3 sg. m.	יֵשֵׁב		יוֹשֵׁב	
Waw cons. imp.	וַיֵּשֶׁב		וַיּוֹשֶׁב	
Waw cons. pf.	וְיָשַׁבְתָּ			
Imperative				
sing. 2 m.	שֵׁב (שְׁבָה) יְרָא	הִוָּשֵׁב	הוֹשֵׁב	
2 f.	שְׁבִי	הִוָּשְׁבִי	הוֹשִׁיבִי	
plur. 2 m.	שְׁבוּ	הִוָּשְׁבוּ	הוֹשִׁיבוּ	
2 f.	שֵׁבְנָה	הִוָּשַׁבְנָה	הוֹשֵׁבְנָה	
Infinitive constr.	שֶׁבֶת יְרָאָה	הִוָּשֵׁב	הוֹשִׁיב	הוּשַׁב
absol.	יָשׁוֹב		הוֹשֵׁב	
Participle active	יֵשֵׁב יָרֵא		מוֹשִׁיב	
passive	יָשׁוּב	נוֹשָׁב		מוּשָׁב

Pe Waw and Pe Yodh Verbs

	Qal	Hiph'il
Cohor. 1 sg.		
Juss. 3 sg. m.	יֵיטַב	יֵיטֵב
Waw cons. imp.	וַיִּיטַב	וַיֵּיטֶב
Waw cons. pf.		
Imperative		
sing. 2 m.		הֵיטֵב
2 f.		הֵיטִיבִי
plur. 2 m.		הֵיטִיבוּ
2 f.		הֵיטֵבְנָה
Infinitive constr.	(יְטֹב)	הֵיטִיב
absol.	יָטוֹב	הֵיטֵב
Participle active	יֹטֵב	מֵיטִיב
passive	יָטוּב	

'Ayin Waw and 'Ayin Yodh Verbs

		Active	Stative		Niph'al
			Qal		
Perfect					
sing.	3 m.	קָם	מֵת	בּוֹשׁ	נָקוֹם
	3 f.	קָמָה	מֵתָה	בּוֹשָׁה	נָקוֹמָה
	2 m.	קַמְתָּ	מַתָּה	בֹּשְׁתָּ	נְקוּמֹתָ
	2 f.	קַמְתְּ	מַתְּ	בֹּשְׁתְּ	נְקוּמֹת
	1 c.	קַמְתִּי	מַתִּי	בֹּשְׁתִּי	נְקוּמֹתִי
plur.	3 c.	קָמוּ	מֵתוּ	בֹּשׁוּ	נָקוֹמוּ
	2 m.	קַמְתֶּם	מַתֶּם	בָּשְׁתֶּם	נְקוּמֹתֶם
	2 f.	קַמְתֶּן	מַתֶּן	בָּשְׁתֶּן	נְקוּמֹתֶן
	1 c.	קַמְנוּ	מַתְנוּ	בֹּשְׁנוּ	נָקוֹמֹנוּ
Imperfect					
sing.	3 m.	יָקוּם	יָמוּת	יֵבוֹשׁ	יִקּוֹם
	3 f.	תָּקוּם	etc.	תֵּבוֹשׁ	תִּקּוֹם
	2 m.	תָּקוּם		תֵּבוֹשׁ	תִּקּוֹם
	2 f.	תָּקוּמִי		תֵּבוֹשִׁי	תִּקּוֹמִי
	1 c.	אָקוּם		אֵבוֹשׁ	אֶקּוֹם
plur.	3 m.	יָקוּמוּ		יֵבוֹשׁוּ	יִקּוֹמוּ
	3 f.	תְּקוּמֶינָה		תֵּבֹשְׁנָה	
	2 m.	תָּקוּמוּ		תֵּבוֹשׁוּ	תִּקּוֹמוּ
	2 f.	תְּקוּמֶינָה		תְּבֹשְׁנָה	
	1 c.	נָקוּם		נֵבוֹשׁ	נִקּוֹם

'Ayin Waw and 'Ayin Yodh Verbs

		Hiph'il	Hoph'al	'Ayin Yodh Verb Qal
Perfect				
sing.	3 m.	הֵקִים	הוּקַם	שָׂם
	3 f.	הֵקִימָה	הוּקְמָה	שָׂמָה
	2 m.	הֲקִימֹתָ	הוּקַמְתָּ	שַׂמְתָּ
	2 f.	הֲקִימֹת	הוּקַמְתְּ	
	1 c.	הֲקִימֹתִי	הוּקַמְתִּי	etc. as קָם
plur.		הֵקִימוּ	הוּקְמוּ	
	2 m.	הֲקִימֹתֶם	הוּקַמְתֶּם	
	2 f.	הֲקִימֹתֶן	הוּקַמְתֶּן	
	1 c.	הֲקִימֹנוּ	הוּקַמְנוּ	
Imperfect				
sing.	3 m.	יָקִים	יוּקַם	יָשִׂים
	3 f.	תָּקִים	תוּקַם	תָּשִׂים
	2 m.	תָּקִים	תוּקַם	תָּשִׂים
	2 f.	תָּקִימִי	תוּקְמִי	תָּשִׂימִי
	1 c.	אָקִים	אוּקַם	אָשִׂים
plur.	3 m.	יָקִימוּ	יוּקְמוּ	יָשִׂימוּ
	3 f.	תְּקִמְנָה¹	תוּקַמְנָה	תְּשִׂמְנָה²
	2 f.	תָּקִימוּ	תוּקְמוּ	תָּשִׂימוּ
	2 f.	תְּקִמְנָה	תוּקַמְנָה	תְּשִׂמְנָה²
	1 c.	נָקִים	נוּקַם	נָשִׂים

1. Or, תְּקִימֶינָה   2. Or, תְּשִׂימֶינָה

'Ayin Waw and 'Ayin Yodh Verbs

Qal

	Active	Stative		Niph'al
Cohor. 1 sg.	אָקוּמָה	אֱמוּתָה	אֵבוֹשָׁה	
Juss. 3 sg. m.	יָקֹם	יָמֹת	יֵבוֹשׁ	
Waw cons. imp.	וַיָּקָם	וַיָּמָת	וַיֵּבוֹשׁ	
Waw cons. pf.	וְקַמְתָּ			
Imperative				
sing. 2 m.	קוּם	מֻת	בּוֹשׁ	הִקּוֹם
2 f.	קוּמִי	etc.	בּוֹשִׁי	הִקּוֹמִי
plur. 2 m.	קוּמוּ		בּוֹשׁוּ	הִקּוֹמוּ
2 f.	קֹמְנָה		בֹּשְׁנָה	הִקָּמְנָה
Infinitive constr.	קוּם	מוּת	בּוֹשׁ	הִקּוֹם
absol.	קוֹם	מוֹת	בּוֹשׁ	נָקוֹם
Participle active	קָם	מֵת	בּוֹשׁ	־נָקוֹם
passive	קוּם			

1. fem. נְקוֹמָה

'Ayin Waw and 'Ayin Yodh Verbs

	Hiph'il	Hoph'al	'Ayin Yodh Verb Qal
Cohor. 1 sg.	אָקִימָה		אָשִׂימָה
Juss. 3 sg. m.	יָקֵם		יָשֵׂם
Waw cons. imp.	וַיָּקֶם		וַיָּשֶׂם
Waw cons. pf.	וַהֲקִימֹתָ		וְשַׂמְתָּ
Imperative			שִׂים
sing. 2 m.	הָקֵם		
2 f.	הָקִימִי		שִׂימִי
plur. 2 m.	הָקִימוּ		שִׂימוּ
2 f.	הָקֵמְנָה		
Infinitive constr.	הָקִים	הוּקַם	שִׂים
absol.	הָקֵם		שׂוֹם
Participe active	מֵקִים		שָׂם
passive		מוּקָם	

DOUBLE 'AYIN VERBS

Qal

		Active		Stative	
Perfect					
sing.	3m.	סַב	סָבַב	קַל	מַל
	3 f.	סַבָּה	סָבְבָה	קָלָה	etc.
	2 m.		סַבּוֹתָ	קַלּוֹתָ	
	2 f.		סַבּוֹת	קַלּוֹת	
	1 c.		סַבּוֹתִי	קַלּוֹתִי	
plur.	3 c.	סַבּוּ	סָבְבוּ	קַלּוּ	
	2 m.		סַבּוֹתֶם	קַלּוֹתֶם	
	2 f.		סַבּוֹתֶן	קַלּוֹתֶן	
	1 c.		סַבּוֹנוּ	קַלּוֹנוּ	
Imperfect					
sing.	3 m.	יָסֹב	יִסֹּב	יֵקַל	יֵמַל
	3 f.	תָּסֹב	תִּסֹּב	תֵּקַל	תֵּמַל
	2 m.	תָּסֹב	תִּסֹּב	תֵּקַל	תֵּמַל
	2 f.	תָּסֹבִּי	תִּסְּבִי	תֵּקַלִּי	תִּמְּלִי
	1 c.	אָסֹב	אֶסֹּב	אֵקַל	אֵמַל
plur.	3 m.	יָסֹבּוּ	יִסְּבוּ	יֵקַלּוּ	יִמְּלוּ
	3 f.	תְּסֻבֶּינָה	תִּסֹּבְנָה	תְּקַלֶּינָה	תִּמַּלְנָה
	2 m.	תָּסֹבּוּ	תִּסְּבוּ	תֵּקַלּוּ	תִּמְּלוּ
	2 f.	תְּסֻבֶּינָה	תִּסֹּבְנָה	תְּקַלֶּינָה	תְּקַלֶּינָה
	1 c.	נָסֹב	נִסֹּב	נֵקַל	נֵמַל

Double 'Ayin Verbs

		Niph'al	Hiph'il	Hoph'al
Perfect				
sing.	3 m.	נָסַב	הֵסַב	הוּסַב
	3 f.	נָסַבָּה	הֵסַבָּה	הוּסַבָּה
	2 m.	נְסַבּוֹתָ	הֲסִבּוֹתָ	הוּסַבּוֹתָ
	2 f.	נְסַבּוֹת	הֲסִבּוֹת	etc.
	1 c.	נְסַבּוֹתִי	הֲסִבּוֹתִי	
plur.	3 c.	נָסַבּוּ	הֵסַבּוּ	
	2 m.	נְסַבּוֹתֶם	הֲסִבּוֹתֶם	
	2 f.	נְסַבּוֹתֶן	הֲסִבּוֹתֶן	
	1 c.	נְסַבּוֹנוּ	הֲסִבּוֹנוּ	
Imperfect				
sing.	3 m.	יִסַּב יַסַּב	יָסֵב יַסֵּב	יוּסַב יֻסַּב
	3 f.	תִּסַּב	תָּסֵב	תּוּסַב
	2 m.	תִּסַּב	תָּסֵב	תּוּסַב
	2 f.	תִּסַּבִּי	תָּסֵבִּי	etc.
	1 c.	אֶסַּב	אָסֵב	
plur.	3 m.	יִסַּבּוּ יַסַּבּוּ	יָסֵבּוּ	
	3 f.	תִּסַּבֶּינָה	תְּסִבֶּינָה	
	2 m.	תִּסַּבּוּ	תָּסֵבּוּ	
	2 f.	תִּסַּבֶּינָה	תְּסִבֶּינָה	
	1 c.	נִסַּב	נָסֵב	

Double 'Ayin Verbs

		Qal		
	Active		**Stative**	
Cohor. 1 sg.	אֶסְבָּה אָסֹבָּה			
Juss. 3 sg. m.	יָסֹב יִסֹּב		יֵקַל יָמַל	
Waw cons. imp.	וַיָּסָב וַיִּסֹּב		וַיֵּקַל	
Waw cons. pf.	וְסַבֹּתָ			
Imperative	סֹב			
sing. 2 m.				
2 f.	סֹבִּי			
plur. 2 m.	סֹבּוּ			
2 f.	סֻבֶּינָה			
Infinitive constr.	סֹב		קַל, קָל	
absol.	סָבוֹב		קָלוֹל	
Participle active	סֹבֵב		קַל, קָלֶה	
passive	סָבוּב			

DOUBLE 'AYIN VERBS

	Niph'al	Hiph'il	Hoph'al
Cohor. 1 sg.			
Juss. 3 sg. m.	יִסַּב	יָסֵב	
Waw cons. imp.	וַיִּסַּב	וַיָּסֵב	
Waw cons. pf.			
Imperative			
sing. 2 m.	הִסַּב	הָסֵב	
2 f.	הִסַּבִּי	הָסֵבִּי	
plur. 2 m.	הִסַּבּוּ	הָסֵבּוּ	
2 f.	הִסַּבֶּינָה	הֲסִבֶּינָה	
Infinitive constr.	הִסַּב	הָסֵב	הוּסַב
absol.	הִסּוֹב	הָסֵב	
Participle active	נָסָב	מֵסֵב	
passive			מוּסָב

1. fem. sing. נָסַבָּה

Lamedh He (Lamedh Yodh and Waw) Verbs

		Qal	Niph'al	Pi'el
Perfect				
sing.	3 m.	גָּלָה	נִגְלָה	גִּלָּה
	3 f.	גָּלְתָה	נִגְלְתָה	גִּלְּתָה
	2 m.	גָּלִיתָ	נִגְלֵיתָ	גִּלִּיתָ
	2 f.	גָּלִית	נִגְלֵית	etc.
	1 c.	גָּלִיתִי	נִגְלֵיתִי	
plur.	3 c.	גָּלוּ	נִגְלוּ	
	2 m.	גְּלִיתֶם	נִגְלֵיתֶם	
	2 f.	גְּלִיתֶן	נִגְלֵיתֶן	
	1 c.	גָּלִינוּ	נִגְלֵינוּ	
Imperfect				
sing.	3 m.	יִגְלֶה	יִגָּלֶה	יְגַלֶּה
	3 f.	תִּגְלֶה	תִּגָּלֶה	תְּגַלֶּה
	2 m.	תִּגְלֶה	תִּגָּלֶה	תְּגַלֶּה
	2 f.	תִּגְלִי	תִּגָּלִי	etc.
	1 c.	אֶגְלֶה	אֶגָּלֶה	
plur.	3 m.	יִגְלוּ	יִגָּלוּ	
	3 f.	תִּגְלֶינָה	תִּגָּלֶינָה	
	2 m.	תִּגְלוּ	תִּגָּלוּ	
	2 f.	תִּגְלֶינָה	תִּגָּלֶינָה	
	1 c.	נִגְלֶה	נִגָּלֶה	

LAMEDH HE (LAMEDH YODH AND WAW) VERBS

		Puʻal	Hiphʻil	Hophʻal	Hithpaʻel
Perfect					
sing.	3 m.	נֻּלָּה	הֻגְלָה	הֻגְלָה	הִתְגַּלָּה
	3 f.	גֻּלְּתָה	הֻגְלְתָה	הֻגְלְתָה	הִתְגַּלְּתָה
	2 m.	גֻּלֵּיתָ	הֻגְלֵיתָ	הֻגְלֵיתָ	הִתְגַּלֵּיתָ
	2 f.	etc.	etc.	etc.	etc.
	1 c.				
plur.	3 c.				
	2 m.				
	2 f.				
	1 c.				
Imperfect					
sing.	3 m.	יְגֻלֶּה	יַגְלֶה	יָגְלֶה	יִתְגַּלֶּה
	3 f.	תְּגֻלֶּה	תַּגְלֶה	תָּגְלֶה	תִּתְגַּלֶּה
	2 m.	תְּגֻלֶּה	תַּגְלֶה	תָּגְלֶה	תִּתְגַּלֶּה
	2 f.	etc.	etc.	etc.	etc.
	1 c.				
plur.	3 m.				
	3 f.				
	2 m.				
	2 f.				
	1 c.				

Lamedh He (Lamedh Yodh and Waw) Verbs

	Qal	Niph'al	Pi'el
Cohor. 1 sg.			
Juss. 3 sg. m.	יִגְלֶה	יִגָּל	יְגַל
Waw cons, imp.	וַיִּגֶל	וַיִּגָּל	וַיְגַל
Waw cons. pf.	וְגָלִיתָ	וְנִגְלֵיתָ	
Imperative			
sing. 2 m.	גְּלֵה	הִגָּלֵה	(גַּל) גַּלֵּה
2 f.	גְּלִי	הִגָּלִי	גַּלִּי
plur. 2 m.	גְּלוּ	הִגָּלוּ	גַּלּוּ
2 f.	גְּלֶינָה	הִגָּלֶינָה	גַּלֶּינָה
Infinitive constr.	גְּלוֹת	הִגָּלוֹת	גַּלּוֹת
absol.	גָּלֹה	נִגְלֹת	
Participle active	גֹּלֶה	נִגְלֶה	מְגַלֶּה
passive	גָּלוּי		

LAMEDH HE (LAMEDH YODH AND WAW) VERBS

	Pu'al	Hiph'il	Hoph'al	Hithpa'el
Cohor. 1 sg.				
Juss. 3 sg. m.		יֶגֶל		יִתְגַּל
Waw cons. imp.	וַיְגֻלֶּה	וַיֶּגֶל		וַיִּתְגַּל
Waw cons. pf.				
Imperative				
sing. 2 m.		הַגְלֵה		הִתְגַּלֵּה
2 f.		הַגְלִי		הִתְגַּלִּי
plur. 2 m.		etc.		etc.
2 f.				
Infinitive constr.	גֻּלּוֹת	הַגְלוֹת	הָגְלוֹת	הִתְגַּלּוֹת
absol.	גֻּלֹּה	הַגְלֵה	הָגְלֵה	הִתְגַּלֵּה
Participle active		מַגְלֶה		מִתְגַּלֶּה
passive	מְגֻלֶּה		מָגְלֶה	

KEY TO EXERCISES

Exercise 1

(a) 1. 'thph   2. blnw.   3. qṭlm.   4. slḥyny.   5. mšlkh.
6. 'rbhynw.   7. zphsln.   8. klwthy.   9. çl'ph'.   10. zrghḥm.
11. tlṭm'yn.   12. hwkhl'ym.   13. ḥph'zyq.   14. ṭyr'š.
15. slq'lw.   16. dphṭ'nyn.   17. 'lysmw.   18. ṣmṭšbh.
19. kçph'yl.   20. ḥzqhms.

(b) 1. חטשם   2. לפאש   3. צרמיז   4. סנטחלי   5. תאקלעמי
6. שבוי   7. קפסעטץ   8. דערמאלי   9. פמחטשאנן
10. כרמעסםקי   11. אווענא   12. טרשדמו   13. בגלסחע
14. צהוגלע   15. קמתי   16. אנצעלץ   17. חנבטש
18. תצאנסאם   19. אמינעטו   20. גרקלאמיז.

Exercise 2

(a) 1. lî or lê.   2. mâ or mĕh.   3. kî or kê.   4. šâ.   5. lâlô
or lâlû.   6. mîmô or mïmû or mêmô or mêmû.   7. ḥôlê
or ḥûlê or ḥôlî or ḥûlî.   8. nâmî or nâmê.   9. ṣênû or
ṣînû or ṣênô or ṣînô.   10. lômî or lûmî or lômê or lûmê.

(b) 1. להלה   2. לילו   3. לולה   4. בהנה   5. מולו
6. נילו   7. מותי   8. לילי   9. קינה   10. ליני.

(c) 1. û. 2. ê. 3. ĕ. 4. î. 5. ā or ŏ. 6. ŭ. 7. ê.
8. ô. 9. ĭ. 10. ō. 11. ă. 12. ŏ or ā.

(d)   1.   2.   3.   4.   5.   6.   7.   8.
   9.   10.   11.   12.

(e) 1. בֵּן   2. בֶּן   3. גּוּר   4. מַם   5. אָכַל   6. צָמֹן
7. אִישׁ   8. מֶחֶן   9. אֱמֶת   10. קְטֶל   11. חָשִׁים   12. סֵפֶר
13. גָּדוֹל   14. הוּא   15. שׁוּרֶק   16. מִלְיֻו   17. עָפָר
18. הִיא   19. עֵינֵי   20. אֶבֶן.

(f) 1. 'ādhām. 2. 'ĕrîth. 3. šālôm. 4. mîmê. 5. çāphônâ. 6. 'îr. 7. băth. 8. 'ĕlômî. 9. lānû. 10. măyĭm. 11. qārā'. 12. kôkhābhîm. 13. yĕlĕth. 14. gāmānû. 15. 'ĕlĕm. 16. 'āçûm. 17. yārē'. 18. kōphĕr. 19. šôr. 20. māḥāh.

Exercise 3

(a) 1. ᵃdhōnî. 2. mĭšpāṭ. 3. ṭôbhîm. 4. yĭqbᵉrû. 5. ḥānăn. 6. mălkᵉkhā. 7. ḫᵒlênû. 8. 'āmᵉdhû. 9. ᵉmôr. 10. gᵉdhôlê. 11. kôhᵃnîm. 12. yᵉdhāmēr. 13. lᵉbhābhām. 14. šā'ᵃlû. 15. 'ᵃnāšîm. 16. 'ᵉlōhîm. 17. hĕḥᵉṭî'. 18. tᵉnâ. 19. 'ᵃšĕr. 20. măḥᵃnēh.

(b) 1. שְׁלָמִי   2. יָקְטְלוּ   3. דְּבַר   4. בְּנֵי   5. אֲלֵיכֶם
6. כְּנַעַן   7. יָרְאוּ   8. יַעֲזֹב   9. חֲזָקָה   10. אַחֲרֵנִי
11. הַחֲלוֹם   12. אֲנַחְנוּ   13. מִשְׁמָר   14. בְּרָכַת   15. חֲזָקוֹת
16. בְּעֵינִי   17. אֵלָיו   18. יַעֲשֶׂה   19. עֲדַת   20. בְּכוֹרִי.

Exercise 4

(a) 1. בְּנֵי 2. יִשְׁכְּלוּ 3. קָרֵב 4. שָׂרִים 5. יְדַעְתִּי

6. גָּדוֹל 7. אָדֹם 8. כְּבַדְתֶּן 9. בְּתוֹרוֹ 10. כָּלְפֶם.

(b) 1. הַלֵּי 2. מֶלְקָחַת 3. מְכָב 4. שֵׁגֶר 5. מַלְכְכוּ

6. בְּכֶם 7. לַעֲרַת 8. יִבָּם 9. מִדְבְּרוּ 10. כְּפֶנִי.

Exercise 5

1. לְאֱמֶת 2. חֲכָמִים 3. שָׂרִים 4. מְשָׁחֲדוּ 5. רוּחוּ

6. הֲיֵלֵךְ 7. מֵאֲדָם 8. זָבַח 9. בַּעֲלִי 10. לַעֲבִיר.

As pronounced :

1. lĕ°mĕth. 2. hᵃkhāmîm. 3. sārîm. 4. mĭšhᵃdhû.
5. rûḥû. 6. hᵃyēlēkh. 7. mēᵃdhām. 8. zĕbhăḥ.
9. bāᵃlî. 10. lăᵃbhîr.

Exercise 6

1. הָאִישׁ 2. הָעָם 3. הַמַּיִם 4. הַיּוֹם 5. הַמֶּלֶךְ

6. הָרָקִיעַ 7. הַקּוֹל 8. הַחֹשֶׁךְ 9. הָעַיִן 10. הַבֹּקֶר

11. אִשָּׁה 12. יוֹם 13. הָעָצֵר 14. הָאוֹר.

Exercise 7

(*a*) 1. The prophet is good. 2. The good prophet.
3. The great and good morning. 4. The mountain is high.
5. The man and the prophet. 6. The temple is great and
good. 7. The night and the day. 8. The daughter and
the woman. 9. The man is the king. 10. The gold is good.

(*b*) ‏1. הָאִישׁ הַגָּדוֹל‏ ‏2. הַיּוֹם‏ ‏3. הָעֶרֶב וְהַבֹּקֶר‏ ‏4. זָהָב‏
‏5. הַמֶּלֶךְ גָּדוֹל וְטוֹב‏ ‏6. הַיָּד וְהָעַיִן‏ ‏7. הָאִשָּׁה‏
‏וְהָאִישׁ‏ ‏8. גָּדוֹל הָעָם‏ ‏9. הֶחָלִי וְהַנָּבִיא‏ ‏10. הַיּוֹם הַגָּדוֹל‏
‏וְהַלַּיְלָה הָרָע.‏

Exercise 8

(*a*) 1. Words. 2. A pair of horses. 3. Fathers. 4. The
two hands. 5. The two sides. 6. Old age. 7. Hearts.
8. Wells. 9. Cities. 10. Two feet.

(*b*) ‏1. שָׁלְחָנוֹת‏ ‏2. אֲבָנִים‏ ‏3. שְׁנַיִם‏ ‏4. שׁוֹטְרוֹת‏ ‏5. הַסּוּס‏
‏וְהַסּוּסָה‏ ‏6. אָבוֹת טוֹבִים‏ ‏7. גְּדוֹלָה הַשָּׂרָה‏ ‏8. עֵצִים‏
‏וְאָזְנַיִם‏ ‏9. טוֹבִים וְטוֹבוֹת‏ ‏10. בָּנִים וּבָנוֹת.‏

Exercise 9

(a) 1. I am the man.   2. The great darkness is the
night. 3. Thou art the good daughter. 4. That is a good
man. 5. What is it ? 6. These heroes. 7. What is this
that he has done? 8. That fair daughter. 9. How lofty
is this place ! 10. Is he very powerful ?

(b) 1. אֵלֶּה הָאֲנָשִׁים הַחֲכָמִים 2. הַשָּׁמַיִם הָהֵמָּה 3. טוֹבָה
הָאִשָּׁה הַזֹּאת 4. הָאִישׁ הַטּוֹב הַזֶּה 5. זֶה הָאִישׁ הַטּוֹב
וְהֶעָצוּם 6. מָה־עִיר 7. מַה־הַהֵיכָל 8. הוּא הָאִישׁ
אֲשֶׁר עַל־הַבַּיִת 9. אֲנִי הַמֶּלֶךְ הֶעָצוּם אֲשֶׁר עַל־הָאָרֶץ
הַגְּדוֹלָה 10. אֵלֶּה הַשָּׁמַיִם וְהָאָרֶץ וְהַיָּם.

Exercise 10

(a) 1. In peace.   2. Like Jehovah.   3. For sickness.
4. To Samuel. 5. Day and night are in the heavens. 6. The
king has a son. 7. Bread and water are very good. 8.
From darkness until the day. 9. Dust from the ground
are we. 10. God is in this temple.

(b) 1. בֵּאלֹהִים 2. כַּאֲרִי 3. לִיהוֹשֻׁעַ 4. יהוה הוּא בַּשָּׁמַיִם
5. מִן־הָהָר 6. הַבֵּן הוּא כַּמֶּלֶךְ 7. בָּהָר הָרָם בַּבֹּקֶר
8. הַהֵיכָל הוּא לַמֶּלֶךְ 9. הָעָם הֶחָכָם הוּא בַּהֵיכָל בָּעֶרֶב
10. בַּת וּבֵן לַנָּבִיא.

Exercise 11

(*a*) 1. I have heard the prophet. 2. The woman did not hear the voice in the great garden. 3. I remember the man who shed the blood in the desert. 4. I wrote in the book in this day. 5. These are the bad mares which we killed on the ground. 6. May he keep the good queen in the palace. 7. And behold, the man took this woman for a wife. 8. And the man Isaac was very great in the land. 9. You shall keep the commands which God has given. 10. The man whom God created is good.

(*b*) 1. אֶכְתֹּב בְּסֵפֶר 2. מִי הַגִּבּוֹרִים וְהַנְּבִיאִים הָאֵלֶּה 3. קָרָא

זֶה אֶל־זֶה וְאָמַר גָּדוֹל יהוה 4. אָכַלְתָּ מִן־הָעֵץ 5. יִשְׁמַע

יהוה אֶת־הָאִישׁ אֲשֶׁר לֹא־יִשְׁפַּךְ דָּם 6. הֲלֹא נָתַן הָאֱלֹהִים

בֵּן וּבַת לַנָּבִיא 7. תִּשְׁמֹרְנָה אֶת־הַדְּבָרִים אֲשֶׁר בַּסֵּפֶר

8. בָּרָא אֱלֹהִים טוֹב וָרַע וְיוֹם וָלָיְלָה 9. זָכַרְתִּי אֶת־אֲשֶׁר

שָׁמַעְתִּי בַּהֵיכָל 10. לֹא יִשְׁמֹר אֶת־הַדְּבָרִים אֲשֶׁר נָתַן הַנָּבִיא

לָעָם בַּמִּדְבָּר׃

Exercise 12

(*a*) 1. The good mares of the king. 2. The prophet took a horse belonging to the king. 3. These are the days of the years of the life of the bad king. 4. God set the sun in the firmament of the heaven. 5. He said, I am the servant of Abraham. 6. And in the presence of all the prophets shall he dwell. 7. Thou hast kept the heart of the great king from evil. 8. The people did not hear the words of the prophets of the Lord. 9. The sword of gold is in the hand of the mighty man. 10. You did not remember the words which the sons of the prophets of the Lord spake.

(b) 1. אֱלֹהֵי הַשָּׁמַיִם וַאלֹהֵי הָאָרֶץ ‏ 2. קוֹל הָאֱלֹהִים בָּעִיר

3. עֲצֵי הָאֵשׁ עַל־סוּסֵי פַרְעֹה ‏ 4. דִּבְרֵי הָעָם הֵם דָּוִד

רָעִים מְאֹד בְּאָזְנֵי הַנָּבִיא ‏ 5. הַסּוּס אֲשֶׁר לַמֶּלֶךְ הַטּוֹב בַּמִּדְבָּר

6. הָרַג גִּבּוֹר שָׁאוּל אֶת־נְבִיאֵי יהוה בַּמָּקוֹם אֲשֶׁר יָשַׁב דָּוִד

שָׁם 7. לֹא נָבִיא אָנִי וְלֹא בֶן־נָבִיא 8. אָמַר אָנֹכִי אֱלֹהֵי אַבְרָהָם

אֱלֹהֵי יִצְחָק וַאלֹהֵי יַעֲקֹב ‏ 9. תּוֹרַת יהוה הִיא טוֹבָה בְּעֵינֵי

הָעָם ‏ 10. הָאָכַלְתָּ מִן־הָעֵץ אֲשֶׁר בֶּן יהוה.

Exercise 13

(a) 1. From you. 2. From him, or, from us. 3. After thee(*f*). 4. With her. 5. Before the man. 6. Their(*f*) horses. 7. Their(*m*) mares. 8. Your(*f*) righteousnesses. 9. I have heard their(*m*) words. 10. Your(*m*) hands. 11. To them(*m*). 12. Their(*m*) words are evil in the sight of Jehovah. 13. The prophet sent his sons and his daughters toward the desert. 14. We have heard thy voice in the temple of the Lord. 15. Between me and thee. 16. And I did not pursue after the sons of Jacob. 17. For I have kept the ways of Jehovah the God of Israel. 18. In the book of the kings of Israel and Judah. 19. They have not kept the commandments of Jehovah which he gave to them on the mountain. 20. And all his judgments are before thee.

(b) 1. לְפָנַי ‏ 2. אַחֲרֵיהֶן ‏ 3. עָלָיו ‏ 4. מִמְּךָ ‏ 5. אֲלֵיכֶם

6. לִפְנֵיכֶם ‏ 7. לְפָנֶיךָ ‏ 8. פְּנֵי ‏ 9. יָדֵינוּ ‏ 10. שְׂפָתֶיךָ

11. צִדְקוֹתֵיהֶן ‏ 12. דְּבָרֵינוּ ‏ 13. סוּסָם ‏ 14. סוּסֵיכֶן

15. סוּסוֹתֵיכֶן ‏ 16. בֵּינֵינוּ ‏ 17. תַּחְתָּיו ‏ 18. הַגּוֹי ‏ 19. שְׂפָתֵיהֶם

20. יָדְךָ הַחֲזָקָה הִיא בָּעָם.

Exercise 14

(*a*) 1. Be not (ye) angry. 2. Thou shalt not steal. 3. Speak, I beg. 4. And God said, fall thou down before me, and I will not be angry with thee for ever. 5. Pursue ye after him. 6. Let him not write in the book of the law of Jehovah, the God of Israel. 7. I went and sold the boy. 8. The man forgot the words of the prophet and did not keep the law of Jehovah. 9. And he set him over all the land of Egypt. 10. He will surely keep the law of God. 11. And when the prophet remembered these words he said, Pursue (thou) after them northwards. 12. Ye are remembering the words of God which I spoke in that day. 13. Behold, I am sending the prophet towards the city.

(*b*) 1. תִּשְׁמֹר אֶת־מִצְוֹתַי 2. יִשְׁמֹר אֹתְךָ מִכָּל־רַע בָּאָרֶץ

3. אֵלְכָה־נָּא אֶל־בֵּית הַנָּבִיא 4. וַיַּעַשׂ אֱלֹהִים אֶת־הָרָקִיעַ בֵּין הַמַּיִם אֲשֶׁר תַּחַת לָרָקִיעַ וּבֵין הַמַּיִם אֲשֶׁר עַל־הָרָקִיעַ

5. אֶשְׁמְרָה אֶת־מִצְוֹתֶיךָ 6. הָלַךְ הָלוֹךְ אֶל־בֵּית יוֹסֵף 7. אֶשְׁמֹר שָׁמוֹר אֶת־מִצְוֹתֶיךָ 8. חָדְלוּ לִסְפֹּר אֶת־כּוֹכְבֵי הַשָּׁמָיִם

9. יָרְדוּ מִצְרַיְמָה לִשְׁבָּר־אֹכֶל בַּמָּקוֹם הַהוּא 10. וְהִנֵּה שָׁלַח אֶת־הַיֶּלֶד לִשְׁמֹר אֶת־עִיר הַגִּבּוֹרִים 11. יהוה הוּא שֹׁמְרֶךָ בְּיוֹם הָרָע 12. הַנְּבִיאִים שֹׁמְרִים אֶת־תּוֹרַת יהוה אֱלֹהֵי יִשְׂרָאֵל 13. הַמֶּלֶךְ מֹשֵׁל בָּעָם בָּאָרֶץ.

Exercise 15

(*a*) 1. And Jehovah said unto me, Say unto them, do
not fight.   2. And we rested in that place many days.
3. And Jehovah repented that he had made man on the
earth.   4. And all the great mountains were covered,
which were under all the heavens.   5. The sacrifices of
God are a broken spirit.   6. Thou wilt send to thy servant
an attentive (hearing) heart to judge this thy people.
7. Son of man, I have broken the arm of Pharaoh, king
of Egypt, and behold, it has not been bound up.   8. Thou
hast said, seek ye my face, thy face will I seek.   9. And
now thou art cursed from the ground which the Lord has
made.   10. And Pharaoh hardened his heart and did not
let the people go.

(*b*) 1. וַיִּשְׁלַח הָאֱמֹרִי הַיֹּשֵׁב בָּהָר הַהוּא וַיִּרְדְּפוּ אֶתְכֶם   2. לֹא
תִלָּחֲמוּ אֶת־קָטֹן וְאֶת־גָּדוֹל כִּי־אִם־אֶת־מֶלֶךְ יִשְׂרָאֵל   3. וַיֹּאמֶר
יהוה הַמְכַסֶּה מֵאַבְרָהָם אֲשֶׁר עָשִׂיתִי   4. שָׁפַךְ דַּם הָאָדָם בָּאָדָם
דָּמוֹ יִשָּׁפֵךְ כִּי בְּצֶלֶם אֱלֹהִים עָשָׂה אֶת־הָאָדָם   5. וּבְסִפְרֵי
בֵית־יִשְׂרָאֵל לֹא יִכָּתֵבוּ   6. הֵן שָׁלַחְתָּ אֹתִי הַיּוֹם מֵעַל פְּנֵי
הָאֲדָמָה וּמִפָּנֶיךָ אֶסָּתֵר   7. לֹא יָכְלוּ לִשְׁתֹּת מִמֵּימֵי הַיְאֹר
8. וְאָמַרְתָּ אֶל־פַּרְעֹה כֹּה אָמַר יהוה בְּנִי בְכֹרִי יִשְׂרָאֵל   9. וְשָׁמְעוּ
לְקֹלֶךָ וּבָאתָ אַתָּה וְזִקְנֵי יִשְׂרָאֵל אֶל־מֶלֶךְ מִצְרַיִם וַאֲמַרְתֶּם אֵלָיו
נֵלְכָה־נָּא בַּמִּדְבָּר וְנִזְבְּחָה לַיהוה אֱלֹהֵינוּ   10. וַיְדַבֵּר אַהֲרֹן
אֶת־כָּל־הַדְּבָרִים אֲשֶׁר דִּבֶּר יהוה אֶל־מֹשֶׁה.

Exercise 16

(*a*) 1. And Jehovah said to Samuel, listen to their voice
and make a king for them.   2. And he came to the gate
of the city, and behold there a woman gathering sticks.
3. As for you, you have caused many to stumble at the law
of Jehovah.   4. And behold, their lord was fallen down dead
on the ground.   5. And thou art cast out of heaven with
everyone who does evil.   6. And Jacob said to his sons,
Why do you look upon one another, behold, I have heard
that there is bread in Egypt.   7. And they said, we have
walked to and fro in the earth, and behold, all the earth
is still.   8. She is the city to be visited by the hand of
Jehovah the God of Israel.   9. And as the prophet heard
these words he took courage.   10. I saw the wicked buried
and they were forgotten in the city where they had so done.

(*b*) 1. בָּא אִישׁ מֵהָעָם לְהַשְׁחִית אֶת־הַמֶּלֶךְ.   2. בָּאתָ אֵלַי לְהַזְכִּיר
אֶת־עֲוֺנִי וּלְהָמִית אֶת־בְּנִי.   3. אֵלֶּה הַמְּאוֹרֹת בִּרְקִיעַ הַשָּׁמַיִם
לְהַבְדִּיל בֵּין הַיּוֹם וּבֵין הַלָּיְלָה.   4. וְהָשְׁכַּב בְּקִבְרוֹ בַּמָּקוֹם
אֲשֶׁר נָתַן הַמֶּלֶךְ לוֹ.   5. וַיֹּאמֶר יְהוֹשֻׁעַ אֶל־הָעָם הִתְקַדְּשׁוּ כִּי
יהוה בַּמָּקוֹם הַזֶּה.   6. מָשַׁלְךָ רֹאשׁ עַל־הָאֲדָמָה בְּיַד הַגִּבּוֹר
7. וַיִּשְׁמַע אֶת־קוֹל יהוה מִתְהַלֵּךְ בַּגָּן.   8. וַיִּתְחַבְּאוּ הָאָדָם
וְאִשְׁתּוֹ מִפְּנֵי יהוה אֱלֹהִים בְּתוֹךְ עֲצֵי הַגָּן.   9. וַיֹּאמֶר פַּרְעֹה
הֵן רַבִּים עַם הָאָרֶץ וְהִשְׁבַּתֶּם אֹתָם בִּמָּקוֹם הַזֶּה.   10. וַיִּתְנַבְּאוּ
עַד־הָעֶרֶב וְאֵין־קוֹל.

Exercise 17

(a) 1. Two feet. 2. His messengers. 3. Their years. 4. Your places. 5. In his heart. 6. Thy(f) calf. 7. Our counsels. 8. Their (m) women. 9. Their (m) waters. 10. Their (f) oxen. 11. Thy (m) handmaidens. 12. Your (m) mouth. 13. Their (f) cities. 14. My vineyard. 15. Two knees.

(b) 1. עֵינַיִם 2. אָזְנַיִם 3. יְדֵיהֶם 4. בִּרְכַתְכֶם 5. דִּבְרֵיהֶם

6. אֲחִיכֶם 7. בָּתֵּיהֶן 8. בְּנֹתֵיהֶם 9. אָחַי 10. רָאשֵׁיהֶם

11. צִדְקוֹ 12. עֶגְלֵיהֶם 13. גְּדֹלִי 14. מַלְכְּכֶם 15. חֲיָלֵינוּ.

Exercise 18

(a) 1. Younger than his brother. 2. David is the greatest of his brothers. 3. His youngest son. 4. The most servile slave. 5. I will be greater than thou. 6. I am taller than he. 7. One of thy tribes. 8. His three sons. 9. On the fifteenth day. 10. The eighteenth year of Solomon. 11. In the second year of Pekah. 12. In the twelfth month in the third year. 13. In the eighteenth year of the king of Israel. 14. Those two. 15. Two by two.

(b) 1. טוֹב מִזָּהָב 2. בְּנוֹ הַקְּטַנָּה 3. גָּבֹהַּ הוּא מֵאִשְׁתּוֹ

4. מִגְּדוֹלָם וְעַד־קְטַנָּם 5. יֶאֱהַב יַעֲקֹב אֶת־רָחֵל מִלֵּאָה

6. לֹא־טוֹב אָנֹכִי מֵאֲבֹתָי 7. שְׁנֵי הֶהָרִים 8. שְׁלֹשׁ בְּנוֹתֶיהָ

9. חֲמִשָּׁה עָשָׂר בָּנִים 10. שְׁתַּיִם וְשִׁשִּׁים שָׁנָה 11. עֶשְׂרִים

12. אַחַת עֶשְׂרֵה שָׁנָה 13. הָאָרֶץ or וּשְׁנָה וּשְׁנָה וְעֶשְׂרִים

14. הַחֹדֶשׁ הָעֲשִׂירִי 15. בַּשָּׁנָה הַשֵּׁנִית.

Exercise 19

(a) 1. He will seek me.   2. Our keeping, or, keeping us.
3. He will make me king.   4. They (m) will keep you (f).
5. You (f) have kept me.   6. Thou (f) hast kept me.   7. He
has kept them (f).   8. After they had made a covenant.
9. We have sought thee in the temple.   10. Seek him
in the morning.   11. When he kept thy words.   12. Make
him king over this people.   13. He who justifies me is God.
14. He will destroy me in that day.   15. For those who
honour me I will honour.

(b) 1. הִמְלִיכַתְנִי   2. שְׁמַרְתִּיךְ   3. שְׁמָרוּם   4. הִמְלִיכֵנִי   5. יְבַקְשֵׁנִי

6. בְּקַשְׁתּוּנִי   7. שְׁמָרוּךְ   8. בְּשָׁמְרֵךְ   9. כִּזְכֹר הָאִישׁ אֶת־

תּוֹרָתֶךָ   10. בַּיּוֹם פָּקְדִי אֹתָם   11. יְכַבְּדֵנִי בָּעִיר הַהִיא

12. אֶשְׁפְּטֵךְ כִּדְרָכַיִךְ   13. שְׁלָחַתְנִי אֱלֹהִים לִפְנֵיכֶם   14. בְּקַשְׁהוּ

בְּכָל־לְבָבְכֶם   15. הַמֹּצְאַתְנִי אוֹיְבִי.

Exercise 20

(*a*) 1. And he said to me, Son of man, stand upon thy feet and I will speak with thee. 2. I will serve thee seven years for Rachel thy younger daughter. 3. And the elders of his city will send and take him from there, and will give him into the hand of the king. 4. Thus saith Jehovah unto the men of Anathoth who are seeking thy life, saying, Do not prophesy in the name of Jehovah. 5. And Pharaoh dreamed and behold he stood by the river. 6. And Jonathan spoke good of David unto Saul his father, and said unto him, Let not the king sin against his servant. 7. And thou shalt serve thine enemies which Jehovah shall send against thee. 8. In the day of evil I will call upon thee, for thou wilt answer me. 9. Thou hast not allowed me to kiss my sons and my daughters. 10. And he divided himself against them by night, he and his servants.

(*b*) 1. תַּעַבְדוּן אֶת־אֱלֹהִים עַל־הָהָר הַזֶּה   2. וְאַתָּה בֶּן־אָדָם הִנָּבֵא אֶל־הָרֵי יִשְׂרָאֵל   3. וַיַּחַלְמוּ חֲלוֹם בְּלַיְלָה אֶחָד

4. וַיֹּאמֶר וְשׁוּב הֲלֹם כָּל הָעָם   5. כִּי הַמָּקוֹם אֲשֶׁר אַתָּה עֹמֵד עָלָיו אַדְמַת־קֹדֶשׁ הִיא   6. וְלֹא תֶחֱטָא אֶת־הָאָרֶץ אֲשֶׁר יהוה אֱלֹהֶיךָ נֹתֵן לְךָ נַחֲלָה   7. כֹּה אָמַר יהוה שַׁלַּח אֶת־עַמִּי וְיַעַבְדֻנִי

8. וְעָנָה יהוה וְאָמַר לְעַמּוֹ הִנְנִי שֹׁלֵחַ לָכֶם לֶחֶם בַּמִּדְבָּר   9. בְּכָל הַדְּבָרִים הָאֵלֶּה לֹא חָטָא בִּשְׂפָתָיו   10. וַיֹּאמֶר אֵלָיו אָבִיו וְשָׁה־נָּא וּשְׁקָה־לִּי בְּנִי.

Exercise 21

(a) 1. And Jehovah said to Moses, Pharaoh's heart is
heavy, he is unwilling to let the people go. 2. And the
earth was corrupt before God, and the earth was full of
violence. 3. And thou shalt speak unto everyone who is
wise of heart, whom I have filled with the spirit of wisdom.
4. And he refused, and said unto his master's wife, Behold,
my lord does not know, and everything which he has he
has given into my hand. 5. And how shall I do this great
evil, and sin against God? 6. As for me, I hate him,
because he does not prophesy good unto me. 7. And if
it is evil in your sight to serve Jehovah, choose ye to-day
whom ye will serve. 8. And ye shall cry out in that day
because of your king whom ye have chosen for yourselves.
9. He will not destroy thee, nor forget the covenant of thy
fathers which he sware unto them. 10. And thou shalt
anoint for me the one whom I shall tell unto thee.

(b) 1. וַיְבָרֶךְ אֱלֹהִים אֶת־יוֹם הַשְּׁבִיעִי וַיְקַדֵּשׁ אֹתוֹ. 2. לֹא יָחַם
כִּי לֹא אָדָם הוּא לְהִנָּחֵם. 3. יְשַׁלַּח אֵת מַלְאָכוֹ לְפָנֶיךָ. 4. וַיִּשְׂבַּע
לוֹ עַל־הַדְּבָרִים הָאֵלֶּה. 5. וְהִנֵּה שָׁאוּל נִשְׁעָן עַל־חֲנִיתוֹ
6. וְדַם־זְבָחֶיךָ יִשָּׁפֵךְ עַל־מִזְבַּח יהוה אֱלֹהֶיךָ וְהַבָּשָׂר תֹּאכֵל
7. אֶבְיוֹנֶיהָ אַשְׂבִּיעַ לָחֶם. 8. וַיֹּאמֶר אֶל־יַעֲקֹב לֹא מְצָאתִיהָ
9. לֹא תִשָּׂא אֶת־אָחִיךָ בִּלְבָבֶךָ. 10. וְלָקַחְתָּ אֶת־שֶׁמֶן הַמִּשְׁחָה
וְיָצַקְתָּ עַל־רֹאשׁוֹ וּמְשַׁחְתָּ אֹתוֹ.

Exercise 22

(*a*) 1. And he went and dwelt by the stream which is before the city. 2. And he arose, and went for his life, and came unto the desert. 3. Arise, eat, for the way is too difficult for thee. 4. And Jehovah said unto him, go, return on thy way towards the desert. 5. And the daughter of Pharaoh said unto her, cause this child to go away, and nurse it for me. 6. And he said, my son shall not go down with you, for his brother is dead. 7. And thou shalt choose from all the people men of valour, fearing God. 8. And the fish which is in the river shall die. 9. Pharaoh will lift up thy head, and will restore thee to the palace. 10. For I am to die in this land, but ye shall go over and possess this good land.

(*b*) 1. וַיֹּאמֶר צֵא וְעָמַדְתָּ בָּהָר   2. לֵךְ שׁוּב כִּי מֶה עָשִׂיתִי לָךְ

3. וַיָּקָם וַיֵּלֶךְ אַחֲרֵי אֵלִיָהוּ   4. וַיִּפְצְרוּ עַד־בֹּשׁ וַיֹּאמֶר שְׁלַח

5. וַיָּמָת הַמֶּלֶךְ וַיּוּבָא שֹׁמְרוֹן וַיִּקְבְּרוּ אֶת־הַמֶּלֶךְ בְּשֹׁמְרוֹן   6. וַיָּקוּמוּ

כָּל־אַנְשֵׁי־חַיִל וַיֵּלְכוּ כָל־הַלַּיְלָה וַיִּקְחוּ אֶת־נִבְלַת שָׁאוּל   7. וַתִּקַּח

הָאִשָּׁה אֶת־הַיֶּלֶד וַתֵּנִיקֵהוּ   8. וַיִּרְאוּ אֶת־שֵׁם יהוה בָּעִיר

9. זַרְעוֹ יִירַשׁ אֶת־הָאָרֶץ   10. וַיֹּאמֶר שׁוּב אָשׁוּב אֵלֶיךָ בְּיוֹם

הָרָע.

Exercise 23

(*a*) 1. The man who curses his father or his mother
shall surely be put to death. 2. Cursed shall you be when
you come in, and cursed shall you be when you go out.
3. May Jehovah lift up his countenance upon you and
give you peace. 4. And she said, drink, my lord, and she
let down her pitcher upon her hand in the well. 5. And
God said, let there be light, and there was light. 6. And
the evening and the morning were the fifth day. 7. For
they weep unto me saying, give us flesh. 8. And his
disease was very grievous, so that there was no breath
left in him. 9. For behold, on the city which is called by
my name I am beginning to do evil in this day. 10. And
God saw that it was good.

(*b*) 1. וַיֹּאמֶר אֵלֶיהָ אַל־תִּירְאִי בֹּאִי עֲשִׂי כִדְבָרֵךְ 2. וַיִּקְרְאוּ
בְשֵׁם־אֱלֹהֵיהֶם לֵאמֹר הַבַּעַל עֲנֵנוּ וְאֵין קוֹל וְאֵין עֹנֶה אֹתָם· 3. וַיְהִי
דְבַר־יהוה אֵלָיו לֵאמֹר קוּם לֵךְ מִדְבָּרָה 4. וַיָּבֹא מַלְאַךְ־
יהוה אֶל הָאִשָּׁה וַיֹּאמֶר אֵלֶיהָ הִנֵּה־נָא לֹא יָלַדְתְּ וְהָרִית בֵּן
5. יְהִי מְאֹרֹת בִּרְקִיעַ הַשָּׁמָיִם 6. פְּרוּ וּרְבוּ וּמִלְאוּ אֶת־הָאָרֶץ
7. וַיֹּאמֶר אֶל־יוֹסֵף הִנֵּה אָנֹכִי מֵת וְהָיָה אֱלֹהִים עִמָּכֶם וְהֵשִׁיב
אֶתְכֶם אֶל־אֶרֶץ אֲבֹתֵיכֶם 8. וְשָׁמַרְתָּ אֶת־כָּל־אֲשֶׁר אָנֹכִי
מְצַוְּךָ הַיּוֹם 9. וַיַּעַל וַיֵּבֹט אֶל־הַיָּם 10. וַיַּעַשׂ הַמֶּלֶךְ כְּכָל־
אֲשֶׁר צִוָּה אֹתוֹ אֱלֹהִים.

INDEX

NEW TESTAMENT GREEK

D. F. HUDSON

A practical and lively introduction to *Koine*, the common Greek language of the First Century AD in which the New Testament was written.

This book is divided into a series of graded lessons and exercises in which the student is progressively introduced to the grammar, vocabulary and sentence structures of the language. It is designed both for the ordinary reader and the theology student as an invaluable and enjoyable aid to a deeper understanding of the Scriptures.

TEACH YOURSELF BOOKS

ANCIENT GREEK
A Foundation Course

F. KINCHIN SMITH and T. W. MELLUISH

This foundation course in ancient Greek provides an original and stimulating introduction to the language for all those deterred by the austerity of traditional courses.

The book focuses on learning to read original Greek. Simple passages are used from the very beginning to illustrate grammar points and introduce new vocabulary. The close connection between English and Greek is stressed, and the reader should finish the book with a sufficient understanding of the language to approach the wealth of ancient Greek literature with confidence and enjoyment.

TEACH YOURSELF BOOKS

LATIN
A Complete Course

GAVIN BETTS

A comprehensive introduction, enriched with authentic Latin poetry and prose passages, to help the beginner approach Latin translation and reading with confidence.

This lively and clearly structured course progresses in easily assimilated stages and assumes no prior knowledge of Latin or of grammatical terms. Each of the units has two sections, the first utilising well-chosen examples to explain new grammar, the second containing carefully graded Latin sentences and passages. Where appropriate, a third section is included, either to introduce the reader to a topic of interest for Latin or Roman studies, or to give additional reading which introduces some of the most famous Roman authors. Revision exercises are provided after every third unit.

Grammatical tables, a key to all exercises, an extensive Latin–English vocabulary and an index are provided at the end of the book.

TEACH YOURSELF BOOKS